A TREASURY
OF SAINTS

A TREASURY OF SAINTS

100 Saints: Their Lives and Times

Malcolm Day

CHARTWELL
BOOKS, INC.

A QUARTO BOOK

This edition published in 2012 by
Chartwell Books, Inc.
A division of Book Sales, Inc.
276 Fifth Avenue, Suite 206
New York, New York 10001
USA

ISBN: 978-0-7858-2984-3

QUAR.SAN2

Conceived, designed, and produced by
Quarto Publishing plc
The Old Brewery
6 Blundell Street
London
N7 9BH

Senior Project Editor Tracie Lee
Senior Art Editor Elizabeth Healey
Designer Tania Field
Editor Andy Armitage
Picture Research Image Select International
Proofreader Anne Plume
Indexer Dorothy Frame

Art Director Moira Clinch
Publisher Piers Spence

Color separation in Hong Kong by
Modern Age Repro House Limited
Printed in China by
1010 Printing International Ltd.

9 8 7 6 5 4 3 2 1

Contents

INTRODUCTION

Saints are the timeless celebrities of the spiritual world. Their influence at the popular level has been inestimable in sustaining the Christian faith. Through bad times and good, devotees have sought comfort and guidance from these holy embodiments of virtue, who once strove to imitate the perfection of Christ.

Yet the idea of sainthood is not entirely free of contention. Roman Catholics will pray to these heavenly agents to plead their cause with God, whereas Protestants believe that only the apostles qualify for such status by virtue of their unique relationship to Christ. Whatever the denominational hue, though, all find in the lives of the saints a great source of inspiration—a fact not lost on Pope John Paul II, who has sanctified and beatified more candidates for sainthood than all his predecessors put together.

SAINTHOOD AS AN INSTITUTION

The practice of declaring devout individuals to be saints has its roots in the third and fourth centuries, when Christian communities began to venerate their founders. Every place where Christians could be found would have a patron saint to protect and guide the daily lives of its inhabitants. Belief in the Middle Ages that these holy men and women had the power to intercede on behalf of those who prayed for their blessing was affirmed by reports of miracles connected with the saint's tomb or relics. In time, patron saints were dedicated to all occupations and conditions. Today, whatever one's concern—be it work, health, safety, relationships, or even such lesser worries as lost keys—there is a saint to be invoked for help.

STEPS TO SANCTITY

Official Roman Catholic doctrine says that everyone who has reached Heaven is a saint, and that the conferring of sainthood, or canonization, is simply the Church's way of announcing that the individual is definitely enjoying the delights of Paradise, having convinced the Vatican of his or her "heroic virtue." The examining process is a lengthy one, lasting up to 30 years. To be considered for sainthood, the person must have lived an exemplary life, displaying the four cardinal virtues of prudence, temperance, fortitude, and justice, as well as the more spiritual virtues of faith, hope, and charity. A dossier documenting the individual's life is assembled and sent to the Vatican, which has been processing applications since 1588. Cardinals and experts examine the dossier and decide whether the candidate showed "heroic virtue." If so, the process of sanctification may begin.

There are two stages. A miraculous cure must be attributed to the candidate since his or her death. If the cure is full and confirmed as scientifically inexplicable by medical experts, the first stage of sainthood, known as beatification, or the state of being "Blessed," is achieved. Then one more miracle is required for the revered person to become eligible for canonization, a decision that rests with the pope of the day.

A SELECT TREASURY

The following 100 saints were chosen to cover as broadly as possible all aspects of life. Some are Doctors of the Church; others led interesting and exemplary lives; some founded famous religious orders; others made great sacrifices for the benefit of others. Some, as in the case of St. Christopher and St. George, have had their status reduced by the Vatican from universal to local veneration because they are considered to be more legendary than historical, yet they still command huge popular appeal.

Cross-references in the text point the reader to other entries that are thematically relevant. For example, St. Martin of Tours, in "Professions and Occupations," is patron saint of soldiers and is cross-referred to St. George, also a patron to soldiers.

FEAST DAYS

The Roman Catholic Church provides an official list of saints' feast days, (usually the day of their death, or "birthday," in Heaven). A saint whose veneration is celebrated only in local regions or cultures will not appear on the official calendar.

TOP LEFT *Variation on St. Sebastian, icon to the persecuted.*
LEFT *St. Isidore, patron saint of farmers and agricultural workers.*
CENTER *Bold St. Boniface, who took Christ to Germany.*
RIGHT *St. Patrick, who freed Ireland of Snakes.*

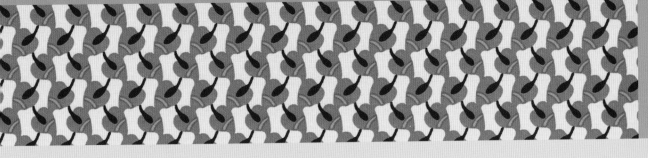

CHAPTER 1

FAMILY AND HOME

ANNE (FIRST CENTURY)

FEAST DAY:	*July 26*
SYMBOLS IN ART:	*Lily, holding infant Mary*
PATRONAGE:	*Housewives, childless couples, pregnancy, women in labor, grandparents, cabinet makers, Canada*
PAINTINGS:	*Bondone, Giotto di,* Annunciation to St. Anne *and* Meeting at the Golden Gate*; Dürer, Albrecht,* St. Anne with the Virgin and Child
PROFILE:	*Mother of the Virgin Mary*

ABOVE *A 15th-century French marble statue of St. Anne holding the infant Mary.*

ALL THAT IS KNOWN OF ANNE, the grandmother of Jesus, is derived from a second-century apocryphal *Book of James* ("brother" of Jesus) which professes to reveal matters leading up to the birth of the Virgin Mary. According to this account, Anne was married to Joachim, a member of the respectable priestly class of Levites. Their relationship was in every way virtuous and happy except that they remained childless. Bearing in mind that the principal purpose of Jewish marriage in ancient Palestine was to bear children, and that not to do so implied divine displeasure, there was considerable social stigma attached to their barrenness, which lasted 20 years. A high priest, for instance, is said to have refused to accept Joachim's generous offering at the temple on account of his unworthiness.

Then, suddenly, each partner received an angelic visitation promising the birth of a daughter. On hearing the news, and convinced of its truth, Anne rushed to see her husband and embraced him at the Golden Gate of Jerusalem. Any misgivings there may have been about God's favor of this couple were dispelled instantly. They vowed to give the expected child to God, and accordingly handed over their precious daughter to the temple priests when she was three years old, never to see her again.

The tradition of Anne's virtuousness grew to a level consistent with her daughter's Immaculate Conception (the doctrine that Mary was born without the taint of "original sin"). As the seventh-century bishop St. John Damascene said of Anne and Joachim, "By the chaste and holy life you led together, you have fashioned a jewel of virginity"—as though, perhaps, their 20 long years of waiting was but a preparation for "giving birth to a daughter nobler than the angels, whose queen she now is."*

By later medieval times there was a good deal of interest in the cult of Anne, and many churches were dedicated to her. In art she is sometimes depicted teaching her daughter to read, and frequently appears in cycles of the life of the Virgin. Her cult flourished particularly in Brittany, northern France, where it replaced worship of the pagan mother-goddess Nanna.

---

*An Exposition of the Orthodox Faith, Bk. IV

JOSEPH (FIRST CENTURY)

FEAST DAY:	*March 19 (as husband of Mary) and May 1 (as "Joseph the Worker")*
SYMBOLS IN ART:	*Infant Jesus, carpenter's square, plane, rod, lily*
PATRONAGE:	*Fathers, manual workers (especially carpenters), the dying, Belgium, Canada, China, Peru, Universal Church*
PAINTINGS:	*Murillo, Bartoleme,* The Holy Family; *Zurbarán, Francisco de,* Rest on the Flight into Egypt; *Rembrandt, Harmensz,* The Flight into Egypt
PROFILE:	*Foster father of Christ and husband to the Virgin Mary*

CONSIDERING JOSEPH was entrusted with supporting the Holy Family, the Gospels provide us with only a sketchy impression of the man and his life.

Although a descendant of King David, Joseph nevertheless lived humbly as a poor carpenter. The first clue to his character comes during his betrothal to Mary. When he discovers before their marriage is consummated that she is pregnant he faces a moral dilemma: He can no longer go through with the marriage, yet he does not wish to dishonor her publicly by renouncing their intentions. Having resolved to terminate the union quietly, he receives an angelic message telling him that Mary has conceived through the Holy Spirit and that it is God's will that Joseph marry her and bear a son.

Thus charged with guiding and protecting the Holy Family, Joseph plays out the role of a caring, responsible father who acts according to his conscience and spiritual direction. After the birth of Jesus at Bethlehem, he takes his family to Egypt to escape the wrath of Herod. On his return to Palestine, his fear of Herod's successor prompts him to go north to the district of Galilee, where he settles in the market town of Nazareth as a carpenter. It is this trade that he teaches Jesus and, no doubt, much of his early speech and manners, too.

We do not know Joseph's age. Medieval painters depicted him as an old man. Clearly by the time of the Crucifixion, when Jesus tells the "beloved disciple" to take care of his mother Mary after his death, Joseph is no longer around to fulfill this role. His cult grew in the Eastern Church from the fourth century, but did not catch on in the West until the late Middle Ages. Thereafter it seemed to gather momentum, and in 1870, Pius IX declared him Patron of the Universal Church. Many churches and hospitals are dedicated to Joseph, and today he frequently represents a kindly figure of fun in children's nativity plays.

ABOVE The Flight into Egypt *(1627) by Rembrandt.*

BLESSED VIRGIN MARY (FIRST CENTURY)

FEAST DAY:	*August 15 (Assumption), September 8 (Nativity of the Virgin Mary), March 25 (Annunciation), February 2 (Purification), July 2 (Visitation)*
SYMBOLS IN ART:	*Wearing blue robe and veil, holding infant Jesus*
PATRONAGE:	*All humanity*
PAINTINGS:	*El Greco,* The Virgin Mary; *Eyck, Jan van,* The Ghent Altarpiece: The Virgin Mary; *Lippi, Filippino,* The Virgin and Child with Angels; *Uccello, Paolo,* Mary's Presentation in the Temple
PROFILE:	*Mother of Jesus; other titles include Our Lady, Madonna, Queen of Heaven, Mother of God, Immaculate Conception, Mediatrix of All Graces*

ABOVE *The Annunciation to Mary by the angel Gabriel that she will bear a son through the power of the Holy Spirit.*

APPARITIONS OF MARY

Many people—and children in particular—have reported seeing visions of the Virgin Mary. Supposed miracle cures are common features, and usually messages about the state of humanity, its suffering, and its lack of piety, are delivered to the world through these seers. Part of her cult includes annual pilgrimages to commemorate her apparitions, for example to Lourdes (1858, France) and Fatima (1917, Portugal).

A S THE MOTHER OF CHRIST, and the only human not tainted by "original sin," Mary is supreme among the saints. Her devotion surpasses all and she is patron to far more conditions, causes, and countries than any other intercessor. Despite this preeminence, Mary is usually a background figure in the Gospels. Her appearances begin with the events surrounding the nativity of Jesus. While betrothed to Joseph, she is visited by the angel Gabriel, who announces to her that, through the power of the Holy Spirit, she will bear a son, Jesus, the Son of God. Her song of praise and thanksgiving, the *Magnificat*, forms a part of Church liturgy. She travels with Joseph to Bethlehem, where Jesus is born beneath a star of great portent, and after a sojourn in Egypt the Holy Family settles in Nazareth.

Mary is depicted as a loving and responsible mother. She is not afraid to question her son when as a boy he stays behind in the temple after she and Joseph have departed. Although she does not always understand the purpose of his actions or of his more enigmatic utterances—such as his response at the wedding of Cana to her observation that the wine has run out—her acceptance of his messiahship is never in doubt. Her sorrow at the foot of the cross in the final hour is the subject of numerous paintings; her plight, by now a widow, prompts Jesus's commission of the "beloved disciple" to take her under his wing after he has gone.

CULT OF THE VIRGIN MARY

From early times, Christians have believed that Mary remained a virgin throughout her life, and the sixth-century doctrine that she was taken up to Heaven in body and soul (the Assumption of Mary) was widely accepted. However, the article of faith that states that God preserved her from the taint of original sin from the very moment of conception in St. Anne's womb (the Immaculate Conception) was debated in the Middle Ages. The Reformers of the sixteenth century opposed the Roman Catholic Church's tendency to glorify Mary, instead emphasizing her humility. The cult of St. Mary has become hugely popular throughout the Roman Catholic and Orthodox worlds and includes such prayers as the "Hail Mary," "Rosary," and "Angelus."

ABOVE The Virgin and Child with Angels
by Filippino Lippi, portraying Mary as an innocent
maiden in a medieval courtly setting.

MARTHA (FIRST CENTURY)

FEAST DAY:	*July 29 (West), June 6 (East)*
SYMBOLS IN ART:	*Cooking pot, ladle, broom, bunch of keys, dragon*
PATRONAGE:	*Cooks, housewives, sisters*
PAINTING:	*Caravaggio,* Martha and Mary Magdalene*; Tintoretto,* Christ in the House of Martha and Mary*; Velazquez, Diego,* Mary and Martha
PROFILE:	*Sister of Mary and Lazarus of Bethany; showed frequent hospitality to Jesus*

JESUS VISITED THE HOUSEHOLD OF MARTHA, Mary, and Lazarus several times, and it is likely that they were good friends of his. A famous scene is described in Luke's Gospel when Martha is busy with domestic tasks while her sister Mary sits with Jesus. Indignant, Martha asks him to tell her to help with the housework, but Jesus defends Mary because she is listening to the word of God. In Christian tradition the two sisters have come to symbolize the twin virtues of the active and contemplative lives. Many of those who have dedicated themselves to worthy causes have championed Martha as their role model.

The only other occasion of Martha's appearance in the Gospels is at the time of her brother Lazarus's death. It is she, not Mary, who first comes out of the house to greet Jesus and, true to the character intimated in the earlier episode, she complains that he arrives too late, it seems, to save Lazarus. Despite the death of her brother, Martha's faith in Jesus remains unshaken, and it is she in whom he famously confides that he is the Resurrection and the Life. As the episode proceeds to its climax and Jesus asks for the stone to be rolled away from the entrance to Lazarus's tomb, Martha—ever mindful of practical matters—points out that by now, the fourth day of burial, there will be a great stench if the stone is removed.

ABOVE *In the biblical scene of the visit to the house of Mary and Martha, Christ regarded both expressions of the sisters' devotion, though different, as equally virtuous.*

LATER TRADITIONS
The Mary of this household was traditionally identified with Mary Magdalene. According to medieval legend she and Martha accompanied Lazarus on an evangelical mission to Provence in southern France, and Martha's relics are enshrined there, at Tarrascon. She is said to have tamed a dragon by throwing holy water over it and wrapping her sash around its neck. She then led the dragon to Arles, where it was slain.

See also MARY MAGDALENE *page 90*

MONICA (332–387)

FEAST DAY:	*August 27*
SYMBOLS IN ART:	*Girdle, tears*
PATRONAGE:	*Mothers, married women, disappointed children, victims of abuse and adultery, alcoholics, widows*
PAINTINGS:	*Gozzoli, Benozzo,* Death of St. Monica; *Verrocchio, Andrea del,* St. Monica; *Vivarini, Antonio,* Marriage of St. Monica
PROFILE:	*Born in Thagaste, Algeria; long-suffering wife, and mother to the wayward young Augustine of Hippo*

IF PERSEVERANCE AND EMOTIONAL ENDURANCE are virtues of sainthood, then Monica was a worthy candidate. Brought up as a Christian, she married a pagan soldier who was debauched, bad-tempered, and very probably unfaithful. On top of this, he had a drinking problem and his protective mother lived with them in their house. But Monica's strength of faith in the ultimate goodness of humanity overcame these obstacles and one by one they subsided. Even her husband converted to Christianity the year before he died.

Widowed at 40, she had borne three children, of whom the eldest was Augustine. She devoted much of her energy to bringing up her children to be Christian—alas, a tough goal with Augustine who, as a young man, looked on her religion with contempt. His relationship with an unknown woman brought Monica constant grief, but she held on to the encouraging words of an unnamed[*] local bishop who assured her, "It is not possible that the son of so many tears should be lost." Perhaps overambitious for her son's success and intent on winning his soul for Christ, Monica pursued him relentlessly from one city to another. On one occasion Augustine is said to have lied about the time his boat departed in order to travel without her.

Eventually, on the advice of others, Monica gave up arguing with her son and instead turned to prayer and fasts. In Milan she became a disciple of the great bishop Ambrose, who was instrumental in finally bringing about the conversion of her son. With great rejoicing, Monica at last felt her mission completed. Augustine wrote in his *Confessions* that on their return to Africa, while waiting at the port in Ostia at Rome, they were joined in blissful spiritual union. He recorded some of her last words:

> *Son, nothing in this life now gives me any pleasure. I do not know why I am still here, since I have no further hopes in this world. I did have one reason for wanting to live a little longer: to see you become a Catholic Christian before I died. God has lavished his gifts on me in that respect, for I know that you have even renounced earthly happiness to be his servant. So what am I doing here?*

Five days later she died from a fever.

ABOVE *A painting by A. Scheffer of St. Monica and St. Augustine depicts the closeness of this mother-son relationship, which endured despite their differences.*

[*]D. Attwater, *The Penguin Dictionary of Saints.*

See also AUGUSTINE *page 140*

NICHOLAS OF MYRA (FOURTH CENTURY)

FEAST DAY:	*December 6*
SYMBOLS IN ART:	*Three bags of gold, miter, crosier, anchor*
PATRONAGE:	*Children, sailors, merchants, brides, pawnbrokers, perfumers, Russia, Netherlands, Greece, Sicily*
PAINTINGS:	*Di Credi, Lorenzo,* The Virgin and Child with St. Julian and St. Nicholas of Myra; *Veronese, Paolo,* The People of Myra Welcoming St. Nicholas
PROFILE:	*Bishop from Asia Minor (present-day Turkey) who is identified with Santa Claus*

ABOVE *An ancient icon of Nicholas of Myra, one of the few saints of the early Christian period to escape martyrdom.*

AFTER THE VIRGIN MARY, this Greek bishop from Asia Minor was the most venerated and colorful saint in all of Christendom. In England alone, some 400 churches were dedicated to him, and there are more artistic representations of Nicholas than of any other saint. Yet, as with many of the early saints, little is known for sure about his life; although plenty of rich myth turned what is thought to have been a holy man prepared to suffer persecution for the truth of orthodoxy into a kindly avuncular figure who bestows gifts on children and saves those in peril by miraculous intervention.

The common image of Nicholas depicted as an old man may be grounded in the tradition that he was one of the few saints to escape martyrdom and to die naturally of old age at his cathedral. A fictitious biography by Methodius in the ninth century created much of the myth of St. Nicholas that made him so popular in the West. When Seljuk Muslims overran Asia Minor and sailors brought his relics to Bari (southern Italy) in 1087, a fanfare inauguration blessed by Pope Urban II sealed his fame. It was reputed that from his shrine the soothing fragrance of myrrh wafted over the poor quarters of Bari (hence his patronage of perfumers). Pilgrims came in droves. There was a time in the Middle Ages when his shrine was one of the most visited in all Europe.

SANTA CLAUS

Perhaps the most popular development of his cult is the institution of Santa Claus. Its origins lay in the Netherlands, where the feast of St. Nicholas, or *Sinte Klaas*, was celebrated and presents were given to children. When migrating Dutch Protestants transported the custom to New Amsterdam (later New York) in the seventeenth century, Nordic folklore about the pagan god Thor was added. A magician riding a chariot drawn by reindeer would visit homes to punish naughty children and reward the good with presents.

A WHIRL OF LEGEND AND CONFUSION

Many of the legends of St. Nicholas stem back to his first "biography." The story of three girls whom he saved from prostitution by throwing three bags of gold to them through an open window became the basis for Santa Claus's largesse, as well as the symbol of three gold balls adopted by pawnbrokers to signify their patronage. A painting of this story was misinterpreted (the bags of money were thought to be children's heads) and gave rise to the idea that he restored to life three murdered children hidden in a brine tub. Distressed sailors off the coast of Turkey have also been the lucky beneficiaries of St. Nicholas's power to save souls.

ABOVE *A 4th-century icon of the Orthodox Church
showing scenes from the life of St. Nicholas.*

ABOVE *St. Jerome (upper left) and St. Ambrose (upper right, in bishop's miter) feature prominently in this altarpiece representation (1499) of the Doubting Thomas and Christ. Ambrose and Jerome were two of four Doctors of the early Western Church.*

AMBROSE (C. 340–397)

FEAST DAY:	*December 7*
SYMBOLS IN ART:	*Pen, whip, beehive, St. Luke's ox, dove*
PATRONAGE:	*Learning, school children, students, bees, wax workers*
PAINTINGS:	*Subleyras, Pierre,* St. Ambrose Converting Theodosius*; Vivarini, Alvise,* Altarpiece of St. Ambrose
PROFILE:	*Bishop of Milan and one of the four early Doctors of the Western Church; known as the "honey-tongued doctor" for his eloquence*

ALTHOUGH THE ROMAN EMPIRE had embraced Christianity as its state religion in the fourth century, the Church was still expected to kowtow to the emperor's word. Ambrose was the first church leader to use his position successfully in altering this balance of power in favor of the Church. He also took a strong stand against heresy at a time when the alternative dogma about Christ asserted by the followers of Arius threatened orthodoxy. As much a politician as theologian, Ambrose used his natural eloquence and classical training as a lawyer to persuade others of his views.

He was born in Trier in Germany and brought up in a noble Roman family. He became a provincial governor in northern Italy but lived in Milan, by then the capital of the Roman Empire. His start in the Church was unusual. When a dispute arose over who should succeed the deceased Bishop of Milan, Ambrose tried to help in overseeing a peaceful election. His gentle and well-modulated address so impressed the crowd in the square that, to his astonishment, it was his name they were chanting as the next bishop. Although professedly a Christian, he was no churchman— he was not even baptized!

Fearful of the situation, he tried to run away and even hid from the public eye. Eventually he was persuaded to take up the challenge in 374, but he had to learn fast. Milan was the center of ecclesiastical as well as secular matters in the empire. At the time, a furious theological debate was raging about the relationship between the Son and the Father in the nature of God. Was Jesus of the same substance as the Father, as the Catholics believed? Or was he like the Father but not equal to him, as the Arians believed? It was a debate that would rumble on, but into this hornets' nest Ambrose, at the modest age of 34, was plunged.

The Roman state was fairly neurotic about its religious beliefs. Pagan gods were generally less favored than they had been in the past but they still had their devotees in high places. Ambrose had to use all his diplomatic skill to prevent a resurgence of interest in them. In the context of his own faith he had to contend with the many new converts to Arianism. The most celebrated occasion was his showdown with the Arian empress-regent Justina, who demanded possession of a church for their worship. Ambrose steadfastly refused to release it, to the point of organizing a sit-in on the site. It was during this highly unconventional form of protest that the idea of hymn singing was introduced as an element of Christian worship in the West.

His power and influence grew to such an extent that by 390 he was able to reprove the emperor for sanctioning a retributive massacre of civilians in Macedonia. Ambrose insisted the head of state do public penance for his actions, setting the precedent that "the emperor is within the Church; he is not above it."

See also AUGUSTINE *page 74,* MONICA *page 15*

BRIGID (BRIDE) (C. 450–523)

FEAST DAY:	*February 1*
SYMBOLS IN ART:	*Cow at her feet, candle, cross made of rushes, flame over her head*
PATRONAGE:	*Blacksmiths, healers, poets, dairy workers, babies, scholars*
PAINTINGS:	*None known*
PROFILE:	*"Mary of the Gael" is the second patron saint of Ireland after St. Patrick; she founded the first nunnery there and is best known for her charity to neighbors*

ABOVE *St. Brigid's modesty was legendary.* The Book of Lismore states, *"She never looked at the face of another man, never spoke without blushing; her desire only to satisfy the poor, to expel every hardship, to spare every miserable man."*

BRIGID LIVED AT A TIME when Christianity was taking root in Ireland. The infant Brigid and her Christian mother, a convert of St. Patrick, were sold as slaves to a wealthy Druid landowner whose interests sometimes clashed with the altruistic spirit that Brigid inherited from her mother. As the dairymaid, Brigid would offer milk to thirsty travelers, and help the poor and the homeless by giving away articles of clothing and furniture belonging to her master. Her standard response to his protests was that Christ lived in every creature. Perhaps unsurprisingly, their relationship deteriorated to such an extent that he could no longer tolerate her under his roof and banished her from his house.

Still young, she took her vows under St. Patrick and went on to found the first convent in Ireland, at Kildare, where she became a nun-cowgirl. At the invitation of bishops, she opened other convents in different parts of the country, contributing greatly to the spread of Christianity. Stories of her miracles emphasize the compassion and charity she showed to her neighbors. On one occasion when some churchmen visited unexpectedly she is said to have changed her bathwater into frothy beer to quench their thirst. Some legends have depicted her as a personification of the Virgin Mary, and hence she is dubbed "Mary of the Gael."

THE DRUID LEGACY

As the cult of St. Brigid (she was known as Bride in England and Scotland) developed, certain aspects of pre-Christian folklore became fused with biographical fact. She was identified with a Druidic goddess of light, fire, and healing of the same name, whose festival was celebrated on February 1. The festival of Candlemas (February 2) has inherited some elements of this old Celtic tradition. Near the shrine at Kildare, for example, a group of nuns used to keep alight a perpetual fire identified with the fire of the ancient goddess. At Candlemas today it is customary for the Irish to make crosses out of rushes and set them above their doors to protect their homes against evil spirits. Brigid is welcomed back each year by rekindling the hearth fire after the house has been cleaned for spring.

See also PATRICK *page 33*

ELIZABETH OF HUNGARY (1207–1231)

FEAST DAY:	*November 17*
SYMBOLS IN ART:	*Bread, roses, pitcher, double crown*
PATRONAGE:	*Baking, lace-making, beggars*
PAINTINGS:	*Collinson, James,* The Renunciation of Queen Elizabeth of Hungary*;*
	Martini, Simone, St. Clare and St. Elizabeth of Hungary
PROFILE:	*Daughter of King Andrew II of Hungary; a nun who cared for the sick*

BORN INTO THE COMFORT of medieval Hungarian royalty, Elizabeth had a fortunate start to life. An arranged marriage for political reasons at the age of 14 to Louis of Thuringia in Germany was a success. The couple bore three children and lived in contentment for six years until Louis died of the plague while joining crusaders assembled in Italy. Elizabeth is said to have run through Wartburg castle shrieking with grief. What happened thereafter is uncertain, but her husband's death proved to be a turning point.

It is thought that for some reason she was expelled from her own home by her brother-in-law, whereupon she decided to renounce the world to join the order of St. Francis. She made provisions for her children, then devoted the rest of her short life to the care of the needy. As a married woman, she had cared for poor families, taking food and garments to them at the foot of the cliff on which her castle-home was built. Continuing in the same spirit, she built and worked in a hospice providing for the elderly and sick. When not actively tending to their needs, she occupied herself with domestic tasks such as baking, spinning yarn, and carding wool. She would clean the homes of the poor and fish in the river to feed them.

ABOVE *A 15th-century painting by the Master of St. Gudule shows St. Elizabeth of Hungary flanked by St. Catherine of Alexandria (4th century) and St. Rosalie (13th century). Emperor Maximus, who put Catherine to death, sits downcast at the feet of the compassionate Elizabeth.*

So much energy did she pour into the selfless service of others, as well as practicing extreme exercises of self-mortification, that her superior felt obliged for her own sake to curb her enthusiasm. He prevented her from giving away her possessions and limited her alms-giving. However, malicious reports of ill behavior from her companions invoked harsh discipline from the superior, a former inquisitor. She suffered sometimes brutal treatment and confessed to living in great fear of him. Nevertheless the punishments yielded no return. As she said of herself, she was "like sedge in a stream during flood time: The water flattens it but when the rains have gone it springs up again, straight, strong, and unhurt."*

Despite the attempt of a Hungarian noble to persuade her to return to her homeland, she refused, saying that all her life and death was now there in Germany. She died soon after, aged 24. Germany's first Gothic cathedral, Elizabethskirche, was built at Marburg to house her relics.

*M. Walsh (ed.), *Butler's Lives*

ANTONY OF PADUA (1195–1231)

FEAST DAY:	*June 13*
SYMBOLS IN ART:	*Book, bread, infant Jesus, lily, torch*
PATRONAGE:	*Lost articles, poverty, starvation, harvests, pregnant and barren women, sailors, travelers, fishermen, animals*
PAINTINGS:	*Titian, The Miracles of St. Antony, three frescoes at Padua; Carducho, Vicente, The Vision of St. Antony of Padua*
PROFILE:	*Franciscan friar and gifted preacher; Doctor of the Church*

ABOVE *Representations of St. Antony of Padua often show him holding a lily (for purity) in one hand, and the infant Christ in the other.*

ANTONY MAY HAVE RAISED A FEW EYEBROWS when he denied his noble Portuguese inheritance to take up the vows of poverty. But even his brethren were surprised when Antony, on hearing how some Franciscan missionaries were murdered in Morocco for their faith, was so filled with zeal for Christian martyrdom that he decided to follow their example and went to evangelize among the Muslims. Though illness there forced him to abandon his mission, he had heard his calling to be a Franciscan preacher.

Antony settled in Italy after his ship landed there during a storm on his return from Morocco. During an ordination ceremony Antony was told to fill in and utter whatever words the Holy Spirit should provide. The eloquence of his sermon amazed all present and thereafter his talents became renowned.

Though he was strong in spirit, his body was weak. Antony died aged just 36 in Padua, the city he had made his home and where his relics remain. Today, his tomb is a popular pilgrimage shrine.

FINDER OF LOST THINGS

Everywhere, St. Antony is asked to intercede with God for the return of things lost or stolen. The reason can be traced back to an incident in the monastery, when his book of psalms was stolen by a novice who had left the community. Antony prayed that it would be found and the thief was moved to return the psalter to him and also return to the order. According to legend, the novice was stopped in his flight by a devil brandishing an axe and threatening to trample him underfoot if he did not immediately return the book. Shortly after Antony's death people began praying through him to recover lost and stolen articles. It is written of him:

> *The sea obeys and fetters break*
> *And lifeless limbs thou dost restore*
> *While treasures lost are found again*
> *When young or old thine aid implore.*

MIRACLES

Three of the most celebrated miracles attributed to St. Antony, who was considered the greatest miracle worker of his time, are as follows:

- At Rimini a horse refused to eat its normal diet of oats for three days. Only when St. Antony held out the Eucharist did the horse break its fast.
- By making the sign of the cross, he rendered harmless poisoned food offered to him by some Italian heretics.
- He delivered a sermon to fish on the bank of the River Brenta near Padua.

See also FRANCIS OF ASSISI *page 38*

CLARE OF ASSISI (C. 1194–1253)

23

FEAST DAY:	*August 11*
SYMBOLS IN ART:	*Carrying a monstrance*
PATRONAGE:	*Television, telephones, embroiderers, needleworkers, sore eyes and eye disease*
PAINTINGS:	*Cesari, Giuseppe*, St. Clare with the Scene of the Siege of Assisi
PROFILE:	*Founder of the order of Poor Clares under the guidance of St. Francis of Assisi*

L IKE ST. ANTONY OF PADUA, Clare came from a noble family. Having refused two offers of marriage, she found that what she desired most was "to leave the world" for such a devotional life as her co-villager St. Francis led. One night she abandoned her home and turned up at the door to his friary. He cut her hair and replaced her finery with a tunic of sackcloth tied about her with cord. From then on her life changed.

BELOW St. Clare is often depicted in art holding a monstrance (receptacle containing the Holy Eucharist) in recognition of its miraculous protection of the convent at San Damiano when it was besieged.

After temporarily housing her at a Benedictine convent, he drew up a way of life for her and a few other devoted women in a house next to the church of San Damiano in Assisi, an order to be called the Poor Ladies, now known as Poor Clares. In 1215 Clare was appointed abbess, a position she held for the next 40 years, during which time apparently she never ventured beyond the walls of the convent. She was joined by her sister Agnes and later by her widowed mother.

Under St. Clare's guidance the community of San Damiano became the sanctuary of every virtue, a veritable nursery of saints. Toward the end of her life, when she was too ill to attend Mass, an image of the service would display on the wall of her cell; thus her patronage of television.

RULES OF THE POOR CLARES

The monastic rules were harsher than any existing elsewhere at the time. Clare was granted the papal "privilege of poverty." This meant:
- living entirely on alms;
- no possession of property, either personal or communal.

Other rules included:
- being dressed barefoot with no stockings;
- sleeping on the ground;
- eating no meat;
- not speaking, except for necessity and charity.

MIRACLES OF THE NUN OF THE EUCHARIST

Clare was known to have a special devotion to the Holy Eucharist. When, in 1234, an invading army was scaling the walls of San Damiano by night, Clare calmly rose from her sick bed and, facing the attackers at an open window, raised a monstrance holding the holy sacrament. As if dazzled, the soldiers fell back and fled. Owing to this incident, St. Clare is generally represented in art bearing a monstrance.

Clare suffered from illness through much of her life. During one such period, she sat upright in her bed and from there is said to have spun a continuous fine thread of silk with which she made dozens of corporals (cloths for the altar) for other Poor Clares convents.

See also FRANCIS OF ASSISI *page 38*

THOMAS AQUINAS (C. 1225–1274)

FEAST DAY:	*January 28*
SYMBOLS IN ART:	*Book, ox, star shedding light, lily*
PATRONAGE:	*Academics, students, universities, publishers, booksellers*
PAINTINGS:	*Sasetta, Stefano,* The Vision of St. Thomas Aquinas; *Lotto, Lorenzo,* Sts. Thomas Aquinas and Flavian; *Traini, Francesco,* Triumph of St. Thomas Aquinas
PROFILE:	*Known as "the Angelic Doctor;" outstanding medieval theologian who drew up a comprehensive theology of the Christian faith*

ABOVE *Patron of academics, St. Thomas Aquinas was often portrayed as receiving inspiration from the Holy Spirit in the form of a dove.*

THE "DUMB OX" WAS the nickname given by contemporaries to this large, quiet man, thought to be a little slow of mind. It turns out that the intellect of Thomas Aquinas matched his physical size. As his mentor Albert the Great perceived, his "lowing" would soon be heard throughout the world.

He was born into an aristocratic Italian family near Aquino in the south, and his university aspirations to be a mendicant friar—who would live by begging alms—were not well accepted. Indeed, he was pursued by his own brothers and locked up at home for a year to make him come to his senses. However, he could not be dissuaded, and he joined the Dominican Order in 1244.

Aquinas vowed to serve God by theological scholarship inspired through deep prayer. He considered that the fruits of the contemplative life should not be kept to oneself but shared with others, and he poured forth a torrent of theological insight, dictating, so it is said, to up to four secretaries at one sitting. At this time Islamic scholars were espousing their religious ideas using the logic of ancient Greek philosophers such as Aristotle. Aquinas responded in kind. He defended the Christian faith and argued against Islam, Judaism, heresy, and paganism. This work was followed by his supreme exposition of the Christian standpoint, *Summa Theologica*, which ran to five volumes and covered such matters as God, Creation, angels, human nature, happiness, sin, and virtues. It has been used by the Roman Catholic Church ever since as its standard statement of doctrine.

In 1272, while in Naples, he received a vision of God that was so overwhelming that he is reputed to have said that all he had written was like straw in comparison to what he had seen. He died soon afterwards of a stroke and probably exhaustion.

A WORLD OF ANGELS

Thomas Aquinas is famous for his system of celestial spirits. He perceived there to be three hierarchies of angels consisting of nine orders. The ninth and closest order to humanity are the guardian angels, defined as essences of disembodied intelligence. He, and other church fathers, taught that every person receives a guardian angel at birth. Their role is to protect and guide their charge and direct the soul to salvation. Although they cannot influence human will directly, they can do so indirectly by stirring up images in the imagination. They can work on the human senses, by outwardly assuming a visible form, or inwardly, by what we term today as intuition. People can communicate their thoughts and wishes to angels only through prayer; angels would otherwise remain ignorant of them.

ABOVE *After Muslim scholars had brought back to Europe the forgotten theories of the ancient Greek philosopher Aristotle, Thomas Aquinas attempted to reconcile them with Christian thinking.*

JEROME EMILIANI (1481–1537)

FEAST DAY:	*February 8*
SYMBOLS IN ART:	*Man shackled with ball and chain*
PATRONAGE:	*Orphans, abandoned children*
PAINTINGS:	*None known*
PROFILE:	*Soldier turned priest who built orphanages and founded an institution for the care of abandoned children*

A friar's simple sketch shows the compassion of St. Jerome Emiliani, who provided emergency relief for starving men, women, and children in medieval Italy.

A T A YOUNG AGE Jerome turned his back on the affluent lifestyle of medieval Venice and ran away from home. He joined the army and served as an officer defending the fortress of Castelnuovo (Treviso) against the League of Cambrai, an alliance of forces intent on breaking the republic of Venice. When the stronghold was captured he was taken prisoner and confined to the dungeon. It was during his captivity there that Jerome, who had no faith until then, began praying to the Virgin Mary. The spiritual experiences that followed and an apparently miraculous escape from prison set him on a new path following the Christian faith. In gratitude to God, he hung up his shackles on the wall of the church in Treviso; hence the symbol of a ball and chain that frequently adorns his depictions in art. Now aged 37, he trained to be a priest.

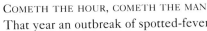

COMETH THE HOUR, COMETH THE MAN

That year an outbreak of spotted-fever plague hit Venice and left hundreds of people destitute. In a single-handed venture of emergency relief, Jerome rented a house with his own money to nurse the sick and accommodate the many children who had been orphaned and would otherwise have starved. He helped women who were pregnant, ill, or homeless.

At night he roamed the city and buried those who lay dead, victim to the plague. After recovering from the disease himself, he resolved to use his inheritance to set up orphanages in six towns, a center for repentant prostitutes, and a hospital in Verona. In 1532 he established an order called the Congregation of Somaschi (named after the town in Lombardy) for the education of children—particularly orphans, for whom he felt the most compassion.

At its height, the Somaschi ran 119 houses in Rome, Lombardy, Venice, and France, and the order still operates today.

GERARD MAJELLA (1725–1755)

FEAST DAY:	*October 16*
PATRONAGE:	*Childbirth, pregnant women, falsely accused people, pro-life movement, lay brothers*
PAINTINGS:	*None known*
PROFILE:	*"Father of the Poor," lay brother of the order of Redemptorists, and famous worker of wonders*

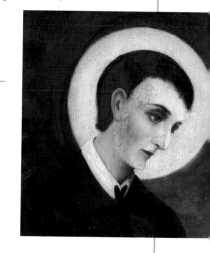

MANY PARANORMAL PHENOMENA were reported of this modest friar, especially in the last years of his short life. Several instances of what were regarded as signs of holiness occurred when he had become the subject of an unusual *cause célèbre* in the quiet world of the cloister.

His father died when Gerard was only nine and his mother reluctantly had to apprentice him to a tailor in order to survive. His heart, though, was devoted to the service of God and in 1749 he joined the Congregation of the Most Holy Redeemer (Redemptorists), founded by his contemporary, St. Alphonsus Liguouri. Despite having weak health, Gerard worked like an ox and was held in high esteem for his charity to the poor. Perceptive and pure in spirit, he became known for an extraordinary ability to read the minds of others. Soon stories circulated of his clairvoyance, even of prophecy, and miraculous healing.

ABOVE *St. Gerard Majella, the saint famed for his prophecy and clairvoyance.*

HERO AND VILLAIN

Special gifts though he had, the daily routine always beckoned. One duty was to open the cloister door to young girls. One girl, named Neria, wished fervently to become a nun but did not have the requisite dowry. By asking of friends, he managed to raise enough money for her entry. Yet after three weeks she was so homesick she decided to leave the nunnery—an embarrassment made worse by the fact that Gerard was a family friend. In thinking of a way to shift the blame from herself, she remembered that he had recently stayed at their home and she concocted a story about his evil behavior with one of her sisters, the details of which she confessed to none other than Alphonsus Ligouri.

The astonished confessor put the matter to Gerard, who surprised him even more by refusing to comment, thus implying his guilt. The issue went to higher levels and soon became the subject of gossip in the friary and in the town. Where previously a sense of holiness had enveloped this saintly friar, there was now suspicion and mistrust. Gerard cut a lonesome figure, pale and withdrawn.

Yet miracle cures were being credited to the alleged criminal now more than ever before. He was frequently seen to be in ecstasy during prayers, normally taken as a sign of divine possession. Perhaps most impressive for the perplexed Alphonsus was an occurrence of the ancient phenomenon known as bilocation, associated with mystics and saints. While in the refectory, Alphonsus suddenly beheld the spirit form of Gerard standing before him in response to his mental summons—yet at the time Gerard was staying in another monastery.

Alphonsus was beginning to look on his subject with a gentler eye. Then he received a letter from Neria, saying she was seriously ill. Fearing God's judgment should she die, she confessed her lie. Gerard was reprieved. Asked why he had not said something in his defense, he replied, "How could I? Does not the Rule forbid me to excuse myself and to bear in silence whatever mortifications are imposed by the Superior?" It is said that throughout the entire case Gerard prayed for his accuser's release from this sin of calumny. Before the year's end, he died of tuberculosis.

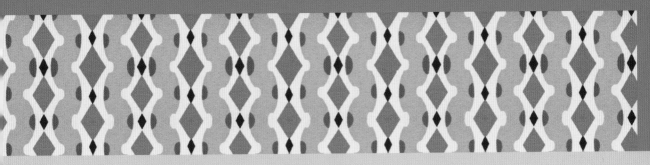

CHAPTER 2

ANIMALS, PLANTS AND NATURE

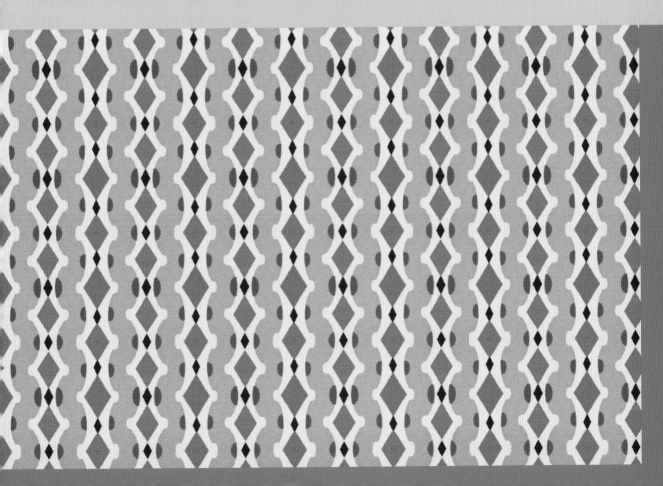

ABOVE *Many monks sought Antony Abbot (left) for spiritual advice. One of his maxims was that the first step to knowing God was to know oneself.*

ANTONY OF EGYPT (251–356)

FEAST DAY:	*January 17*
PATRONAGE:	*Desert monks, domestic animals*
PAINTINGS:	*Bosch, Hieronymus,* Temptation of St. Antony; *Brueghel, Jan the Elder,* Temptation of St. Antony; *Patenier, Joachim,* Temptation of St. Antony
PROFILE:	*Desert hermit and early proponent of the monastic ideal*

FACTS SOMETIMES UNDERSTATED about this saint are his extraordinarily long life—of 105 years— and its crucial turning point when he was just nineteen. Six months after inheriting a large estate near Memphis in Upper Egypt from his deceased parents, he heard in church the famous utterance of Jesus to the rich young man, "Go, sell what you have, and give it to the poor, and you shall have treasure in heaven." To Antony the words came as though addressed to him personally. He went out, sold his possessions and gave the proceeds to the poor. Then, in emulation of an old hermit living in the neighborhood, Antony took up the habit of an ascetic.

He ate only bread and a little salt and drank nothing but water. He never ate before sunset and slept on a rush mat on the floor. Yearning to live a life still closer in union with God and to imitate Christ in the wilderness, Antony at the age of 35 embarked on his famous "flight from the world," which would last for 20 years. His home became a few caves at the top of a cliff in the Egyptian desert. To this barren refuge a friend would bring him bread and water every six months.

THE HOSPITALERS OF ST. ANTONY

❖

The legacy of this nature-loving saint continued through an order founded around 1100, which became widespread over Western Europe. Dressed in black robes with a blue cross, the monks would ring bells to attract alms and then hang the bells around the necks of animals to protect them from disease. A special privilege was given to this order's pigs in allowing them to wander freely in the streets.

THE TEMPTATIONS OF "WILD BEASTS"

It was in this wilderness that Antony is said to have fought the "wild beasts" of temptation, the guises of Satan, as he interpreted them. In a biography of Antony, St. Athanasius recorded his experiences: "It was as though demons were breaking through the four walls of the little chamber … All at once the place was filled with the phantoms of lions, bears, leopards, bulls, of serpents and asps, of scorpions and wolves." [*] The lurid temptations became favorite themes for painters. Some depicted the beasts as if they were rendered tame by this holy anchorite, pointing to his patronage of domesticated animals.

GOD IN CREATION

Antony's interpretation of the true Christian life had won many followers, who sought him out for advice. At the age of 55, he left his solitude to set up a monastery, one of the earliest known in Christendom, where he taught disciples. He lived by gardening and mat making, and until his dying day he looked for God's guidance in the natural world instead of in written matter. When asked how he could manage without the Bible, he pointed to the landscape and replied, "My book is the nature of created things, and it is present when I want to read the words of God." [*]

[*] From *The Life of Antony*

BLAISE (FOURTH CENTURY)

FEAST DAY:	*February 3*
SYMBOLS IN ART:	*Wool comb, two crossed candles*
PATRONAGE:	*Diseased animals (especially cattle), throat sufferers, woolworkers, veterinarians*
PAINTINGS:	*Brandi, Giacinto,* The Martyrdom of St. Blaise; *Niccolo, Andrea de,* St. John the Baptist, St. Blaise and St. Sebastian
PROFILE:	*Physician and martyr; believed to be Bishop of Sebaste in Armenia; one of the Fourteen Holy Helpers*

FOURTEEN HOLY HELPERS

Blaise is one of a group of saints who attracted a cult following from the fourteenth century in Germany, Hungary, and Sweden. The saints were selected on the basis of being effective intercessors against various diseases, especially at death's door, when prayers to them were believed to bring salvation. The other Helper Saints include Acacius, Barbara, Catherine of Alexandria, Christopher, Cyricus, Denys, Erasmus, Eustace, George, Giles, Margaret of Antioch, Pantaleon, and Vitus.

THE SPORADIC PERSECUTION of Christians that broke out in the Roman Empire forced the Armenian bishop and doctor to flee from his diocese in Cappadocia (modern Turkey) and take up residence as a hermit in a cave on Mount Argeus.

ANIMAL SURGERY

During his time as a troglodyte, so tradition says, Blaise would encounter many wild animals. Something about his aura seemed to dispel their bestial instincts and none attacked him. The devout bishop would spend long periods kneeling in prayer, unperturbed by the gathering of creatures at the entrance to his cave. Tradition goes on to relate how the wounded or sick ones would come forward and be comforted by him. He would give them his blessing and dress wounds if necessary.

ABOVE *Bishop St. Blaise, shown here with St. Guerin, is frequently invoked on his feast day to help sufferers of throat ailments.*

Water bearing the blessing of St. Blaise is still given to sick cattle—for example, to those suffering from foot-and-mouth disease. The application of his medical knowledge to animal causes makes St. Blaise patron to veterinarians.

UNDER ARREST

He was discovered when huntsmen, looking for wild animals to use in arena games, found many of them around the cave he had chosen as his hideout. Drawing near, they saw the hermit on his knees in prayer and, thinking he might be a Christian, arrested him. Upon being questioned by the governor, Blaise confessed his faith and was imprisoned.

While incarcerated, he healed several fellow inmates, including a child who was choking on a fishbone. Ever since, on the feast day of St. Blaise, a service is held for throat sufferers who are blessed by having two lighted candles, tied together in the form of a cross, held under their chins.

His martyrdom—by having his flesh torn using wool combs—was the gruesome foundation of his patronage to those involved in the wool trade. Four miraculous cures were recorded at his shrine but his cult did not become widely popular until the eighth century.

See also FRANCIS OF ASSISI *page 38*

PATRICK (C. 385–461)

FEAST DAY:	*March 17*
SYMBOLS IN ART:	*Shamrock, snakes, bishop's crosier, harp*
PATRONAGE:	*Snake bites, fear of snakes, excluded people, Ireland, Nigeria*
PAINTINGS:	*None known*
PROFILE:	*Missionary to the Irish; according to legend, he expelled snakes from Ireland*

PATRICK WAS BORN INTO A ROMAN-BRITISH Christian family near the west coast of Britain somewhere between the Rivers Severn and Clyde. He was captured as a young man by pirates and taken to Ireland, where he was kept as a slave for six years. The experience left a profound impression on him, for after he had escaped back to his homeland he returned to Ireland years later as a missionary, determined to convert the pagan population.

Supposedly trained by St. Germanus at Auxerre in Gaul, he was made a bishop before he undertook the great challenge, in 432. Although there were some pockets of Christianity in Ireland at the time of his landing, most people worshipped the Sun and pagan idols. Patrick had an advantage over the earlier missionary Palladius of being able to speak in the Gaelic tongue, which he learned in captivity. But it was his zeal and commanding presence that won over so many of the inhabitants. On Easter eve he set the Paschal bonfire ablaze on the hill of Slane for all to see the "light of Christ," and confronted the druid King Laoghaire. The power of his preaching drowned out any local protestations and his prowess became legendary.

He spent the rest of his life preaching the Gospel, founding religious houses, and educating the young. St. Brigid was one of his helpers. In 444, Patrick established his episcopal see at Armagh. He encouraged the cloistered life, and subsequently the Irish Church acquired a monastic character with deeper devotion than was maybe evident anywhere else in Christendom.

Toward the end of his life Patrick wrote a Confession in which he saw his life as a spiritual journey. He describes his retreat as lasting 40 days on Cruachan Aigli in Mayo, which became the focus for the Croagh Patrick pilgrimage.

BANISHING SNAKES

According to legend, St. Patrick expelled all snakes from Ireland using a holy staff, and to this day there are no snakes on the island. As patron against snake bites, he is sometimes depicted in art trampling snakes underfoot. Elsewhere he is driving them out wearing full episcopal attire in a reference to God's banishment of the serpent from the Garden of Eden in the Book of Genesis. St. Patrick's striving to rid Ireland of all things pagan and contrary to the message of God is symbolized in the same image.

LEFT *Flanked by fellow missionary saints, Columba and Brigid, St. Patrick blesses the people of Ireland from the summit of Mount Aigli, which he climbed, it is said, to view the fruit of his labors.*

See also BRIGID *page 20,* COLUMBA *page 34*

COLUMBA (521–597)

FEAST DAY:	*June 9*
SYMBOLS IN ART:	*Bear, horse*
PATRONAGE:	*Bookbinders, poets, Scotland, Ireland, protector against floods*
PAINTINGS:	*Weyden, Rogier van der, St. Columba Altarpiece*
PROFILE:	*Irish monk who founded the monastery of Iona; missionary to Scotland; poet and copyist*

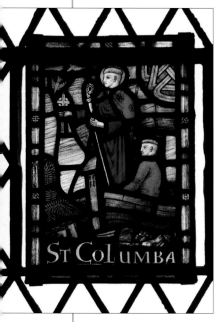

ABOVE *In remorse for his misdeeds, St. Columba braved the treacherous Irish Sea and served a penance of exile among the heathen Picts of Scotland.*

AMONG THE MOST LEARNED of medieval Western Europe were the monks of Ireland. Their discipline and dedication were second to none. Combine these qualities with the artistic tradition of the ancient Celts and the result is the beautiful tradition of illuminating Bible manuscripts, which we still have today in such works as *The Book of Kells* and the *Lindisfarne Gospels*. The foremost of Irish copyists was St. Columba.

Ironically, it was the craft in which he so excelled that, according to his biographer, led to his exile. On finding that his former tutor, St. Finnian, had possession of the first copy of St. Jerome's *Book of Psalms*, Columba secretly set to work in his drafty cell painstakingly copying the contents. When Finnian found out, his demand to take back the copy was upheld by the king who declared, "To every cow her calf; to every book its copy."

Columba, an influential man strong in build and conviction, is said to have been so incensed that a battle between monasteries ensued causing the deaths of some 3,000 men, apparently for no greater cause than his honor.

Filled with remorse, Columba is said to have condemned himself to exile. He vowed to devote the rest of his life to winning as many souls for the Church as were lost on the battlefield. Aged about 44, with a band of 12 fellow monks (one to represent each of Christ's apostles), he sailed away from his beloved country, where he had founded monasteries such as Kells, and braved the tempestuous Irish Sea. He landed at Iona, where he established a monastery that would become the center of northern Celtic Christianity, and whose graveyard future kings of Scotland, including Macbeth, would fill. The relics of St. Columba became a patriotic talisman for the Scots, who carried them to victory against the English at the Battle of Bannockburn in 1314.

CREATURE LEGENDS

From Iona, Columba and his fellow monks set out on missions to the Picts (predecessors of the Scots), and stories circulated of his miraculous powers.

- It was said that he tamed an aquatic monster pursuing one of his companions rowing across a river. Since then the creature, now known as the Loch Ness monster, has been sighted but never known to cause harm.
- He banished snakes from Iona so that people and cattle would be safe.
- On the Isle of Skye, Columba encountered a huge boar in a forest and killed it by power of word alone.
- Knowing he was soon to die, the repentant monk sat wearily one evening by a stone cross. His white horse laid its head on his arm and whinnied in distress. The next day Columba died in peace.

GERTRUDE OF NIVELLES (626–659)

FEAST DAY:	*March 17*
SYMBOLS IN ART:	*Staff with mouse running up it*
PATRONAGE:	*Cats, the recently deceased, gardeners, travelers, mental illness, fear of mice and rats*
PAINTINGS:	*None known*
PROFILE:	*Abbess, mystic, and visionary*

ABOVE *Devotees of St. Gertrude would leave gold and silver effigies of mice at her shrine in the belief that rodents might carry souls away from Purgatory.*

GERTRUDE'S DEDICATION to the religious life was evident at the tender age of 10, when she turned down the offer of a noble marriage, declaring that she would not marry him or any other suitor: Christ alone would be her bridegroom. When her father, Pepin I of Landen, died three years later, her mother built a double monastery at Nivelles, south of Brussels, where she and her daughter retired. Gertrude, aged 20, became the abbess.

She was known for her hospitality to pilgrims and her aid to missionary monks from Ireland. She even gave land to one monk so that he could build a monastery at Fosse. By her early thirties Gertrude had become so weakened by the austerity of abstaining from food and sleep that she had to resign her office, and spent the rest of her days studying Scripture and doing penance. It is said that on the day before her death she sent a messenger to Fosse, asking the superior if he knew when she would die. His reply indicated that death would come the next day during holy Mass— the prophecy was fulfilled. She died at the significant age of 33, the age of Jesus at his death. Her feast day of March 17 is observed by gardeners, who regard fine weather on that day as a sign to begin spring planting.

CULT OF MICE

Her cult spread widely in the Lowland countries and England. As with popular saints, it attracted its fair share of folklore. Most representations in art depict her as an abbess with mice, rats, or cats. Commonly seen running up her pastoral staff or cloak are hopeful-looking mice representing souls in purgatory, to which she had an intense devotion. Even as recently as 1822, offerings of mice made of gold and silver were left at her shrine in Cologne.

An extension of this belief was her patronage of those who had recently died. They were popularly thought to undergo a journey of three days to the next world. The first night would be spent under St. Gertrude's wing and the second under the Archangel Michael's.

Another patronage is to travelers on the high seas. A legend tells of the saint sending her subjects to a distant land, promising that no misfortune would befall them. While they were on the ocean a huge sea monster threatened to capsize their ship, but disappeared upon the invocation of St. Gertrude. To safeguard against any such eventuality, travelers in the Middle Ages drank the so-called "St. Gertrude's Mint" before setting out on their journey.

CUTHBERT (634–687)

FEAST DAY:	*March 20*
SYMBOLS IN ART:	*Swans and otters*
PATRONAGE:	*Sailors, shepherds, watermen, protector against plague*
PAINTINGS:	*None known*
PROFILE:	*Anglo-Saxon monk and Bishop of Lindisfarne*

ABOVE *A halo of eider ducks signifies St. Cuthbert's special affinity with the birdlife of the Farne Islands, in a stained glass window of Durham Cathedral.*

CUTHBERT GREW UP AS AN ORPHANED SHEPHERD BOY spending long days on the pastures of southern Scotland. One night, while tending his flock alone, he experienced a vision: A beam of light shone across the black sky illuminating a host of angels bearing a saintly figure toward Heaven. Cuthbert discovered later that St. Aidan, founder of Lindisfarne Abbey, had died that night. Inspired by the vision, Cuthbert took holy orders at Melrose Abbey two years later aged seventeen.

NATURE LOVER

He briefly stayed at Ripon Abbey in Yorkshire, and in 661 became Abbot of Melrose. However, he liked most of all to spend his time in solitude in the wild archipelago of the Farne islands a few miles off the coast of Northumbria. Following an ascetic practice of the time, he would meditate in water, standing waist-deep for long periods in the freezing sea. It is said that afterwards sea otters would dry his legs.

For eight years he lived as a hermit on the little islet of Inner Farne, where he shared his sanctuary with thousands of birds. He was especially fond of eider ducks, which became known as "St. Cuthbert's chickens." He developed a considerable knowledge of wildlife, and it was believed that the creatures inhabiting the Farne Islands fell under his protection— a prototype conservationist.

Despite his love of observing nature, Cuthbert was a tireless worker, walking long distances to visit the sick, especially when the "yellow plague," as it was called, hit the country. Miraculous healing became associated with his name, and in 685 he was summoned to be Bishop of Lindisfarne.

He had a good head for ecclesiastical affairs, as was shown in his involvement in the Synod of Whitby of 664, at which the liturgy of the Celtic Church was brought into line with Rome. Yet illness cut short his life. He died just two years into his episcopacy, fittingly on Farne Island.

THE BODY INCORRUPT

Eleven years after his death, Cuthbert's body was exhumed in order that it might be enshrined. Miraculously, the corpse showed no sign of decay, a phenomenon traditionally taken to indicate the person's sanctity. In his honor the ornate *Gospels of Lindisfarne* were commissioned. Viking raids in 875 prompted monks to remove Cuthbert's relics to a safer place. After a long period in transit they came to their final resting place in Durham. A Saxon church was built for Cuthbert, which was replaced in 1104 by the present Norman cathedral. Even then, on further examination, the most cynical of skeptics had to concede that the body had remained incorrupt.

GILES (DIED C. 712)

FEAST DAY:	*September 1*
SYMBOLS IN ART:	*Arrow, saint protecting a female deer*
PATRONAGE:	*Forests and woods, fear of the dark, rams, horses, nursing mothers, the physically disabled, beggars, the depressed, epileptics*
PAINTINGS:	*de Coloswar, Master Thomas,* The Death of St. Giles
PROFILE:	*Sage and hermit who saved a female deer from a hunting party*

LITTLE IS KNOWN FOR SURE, but much is written, about this man who acquired a great following in medieval Europe when his shrine in Provence became a stopping point on the pilgrimage route between Rome and Compostela in Spain. He is said to have given his noble inheritance to the poor of Athens, his birthplace, to live in a cave in the forested diocese of Nimes. His impoverishment was such that it was said that God sent a female deer to nourish him with her milk.

One celebrated incident gave root to his fame. One day a royal hunting party was in chase of the pet deer, which ran to its master for protection. As St. Giles held the creature in his arms within a thorn bush that guarded the entrance to his cave, the hounds appeared to become strangely shy of closing in on their prey. One of the hunters took the initiative and shot an arrow into the bush, striking Giles in the leg and crippling him.

ABOVE *St. Giles and the pet deer who, it was said, suckled him as a starving hermit.*

The contrite Visigothic king sent doctors to minister to the hermit, who refused treatment. It is said that the king subsequently visited him several times, as much to ask advice as to offer compassion. Giles's reputation for wisdom and holiness grew and at one point tradition says even Emperor Charlemagne sought him out.

Meanwhile the king so admired him that he had a monastery, later called St. Gilles du Gard, built for his followers, and Giles was made its abbot. After his death his grave became a popular shrine, and many physically disabled people made the pilgrimage to it hoping for alms. Poor houses and hospices were built in his honor in many parts of Europe.

SPANISH RAMS

In Spain, shepherds consider Giles to be the protector of rams. On his feast day it was customary to wash the rams and dye their wool a bright color. Lighted candles were then tied to their horns, and the animals were brought down the mountain to be blessed in the churches. Every year, on September 1, shepherds in the Basque region come down from the Pyrenees wearing traditional dress of sheepskin coats and carrying staves and crooks to attend Mass with their best rams. The event signals the opening of various autumn festivals with their processions and dancing in fields.

ABOVE *Giotto's* Stigmatization of St. Francis *(1300)*
on the mountain of La Verna in Italy.

FRANCIS OF ASSISI (1181–1226)

FEAST DAY:	*October 4*
SYMBOLS IN ART:	*Birds, deer, fish, wolf, stigmata*
PATRONAGE:	*Nature conservation, ecologists*
PAINTINGS:	*Bellini, Giovanni,* St. Francis in Ecstasy; *Caravaggio,* St. Francis; *di Bondone, Giotto, various frescoes; El Greco,* St. Francis Receiving the Stigmata; *Rubens, Pieter,* St. Francis of Assisi Receiving the Stigmata
PROFILE:	*Founder of the Franciscan friars; author of "Canticle of the Sun" (also known as "Canticle of Brother Sun" and "Canticle of the Creatures")*

ABOVE *A 15th-century woodcut of St. Francis receiving the stigmata.*

THIS SON OF A RICH ITALIAN DRAPER was set to become a knight until his growing uneasiness with the plight of the poor, coupled with a salving pilgrimage to Rome, made him question his values. A visionary experience one day in church brought matters to a head. Hearing a voice telling him to "repair my church," the 24-year-old responded with such abandon that in the process he fell out with his father, surrendered all his inheritance, and even divested himself of the fine clothes he wore. A local bishop gave him some simple garments in which to start a new life, married to Lady Poverty.

Francis's "conversion," though, was religious, not social. After raising enough money to literally repair the church of San Damiano in Assisi, Francis set about preaching a new spirit of Christianity. At first he roamed the countryside as a poor mendicant, begging from the rich and giving to the poor. He soon attracted a band of followers impressed by his generosity and humility and the simplicity of his faith, which had no need of the grand edifice of the Catholic Church.

GOD IN NATURE
He did not turn to nature as a refuge from the world but looked on creatures as objects of love that reflected their maker. The sermon to the birds is well known, as is the taming of the wolf of Gubbio. His famous "Canticle of the Sun"* expresses his special affinity with all creation and the yearning he felt for the state of innocence enjoyed by Adam in the Garden of Eden.

Praise to Thee, my Lord, for all Thy creatures,
Above all Brother Sun,
Who brings us the day and lends us his light.

Praise to Thee, my Lord, for Brother Wind,
For air and cloud, for calm and all weather,
By which Thou supportest life in all Thy creatures.

Praise to Thee, my Lord, for Sister Water,
Who is so useful and humble,
Precious and pure.

Praise to Thee, my Lord, for our sister Mother Earth,
Who sustains and directs us,
And brings forth varied fruits, and colored flowers, and plants.

ORDER FOR SIMPLE PIETY
The basis of Francis's rule for the communal life was that its members should live simply, as poor laborers did, in nothing grander than rush huts, with no chairs or tables. Gone were the acts of self-mortification characteristic of religious houses in the Middle Ages. The enterprise was so popular that, while Francis was away evangelizing the Saracens, his order expanded beyond his control. The modest friar, who was no administrator, felt compelled to resign and instead founded a smaller organization.

STIGMATA OF CHRIST
Toward the end of his life, Francis spent a Lenten retreat on Mount La Verna in meditation. It was here that the famous miracle of the stigmata occurred, leaving him with wounds resembling those of Christ's Crucifixion, the first of such manifestations in a saint. The pain, he said, he gladly bore as that issued by God, not man.

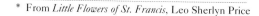

* From *Little Flowers of St. Francis*, Leo Sherlyn Price

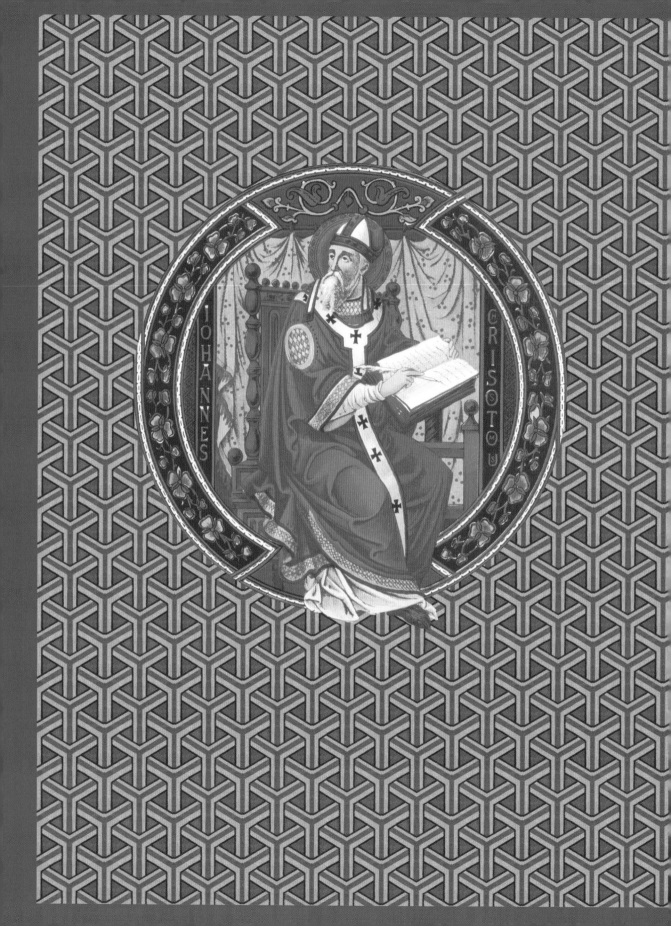

CHAPTER 3

SOCIETY

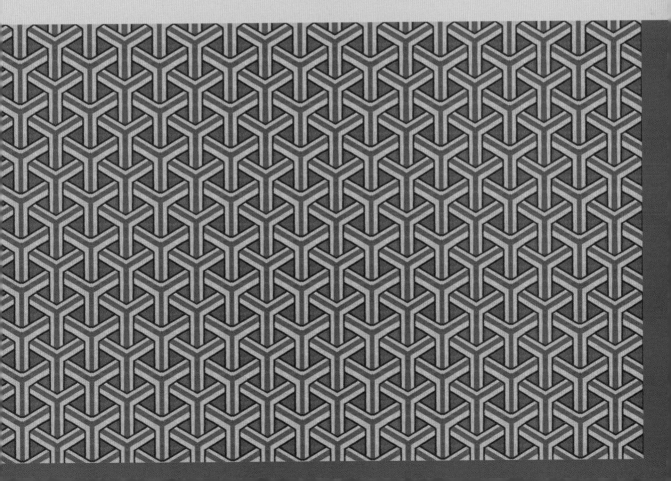

JOHN THE APOSTLE (DIED LATE FIRST CENTURY)

FEAST DAY: *May 6 and December 27 in the West, September 26 in the East*
SYMBOLS IN ART: *Cup containing a viper, book, eagle*
PATRONAGE: *Theologians, writers, publishers, booksellers*
PAINTINGS: *El Greco,* Apostle St. John the Evangelist
PROFILE: *Fisherman and disciple of Jesus; by tradition the author of the Fourth Gospel (in which he is taken to be "the beloved disciple"), three epistles and the Book of Revelation; he is also known as "the Divine"*

LOVE FOR ALL

One of the traits of the early church was its openness to all, irrespective of class, gender, or ethnic background—one of its pioneers was St. John. Despite being Jewish, he ignored the traditional contempt his people held for Samaritans, and confirmed thousands of them in the new faith. The story of the Woman of Samaria, told only in St. John's Gospel, likewise illustrates how prejudice and stereotyping in society can be overcome.

Beloved, let us love one another: for love is of God; and everyone that loveth is born of God, and knoweth God. He that loveth not, knoweth not God; for God is love.

First Epistle of John, chapter 4, verses 7–8 [KSV]

THESE FAMOUS VERSES sum up the message of St. John, whose repeated urgings of his followers to love one another echoed Christ's commandment. Living at a time when much was speculated about the meaning of Christ's incarnation on Earth, John encapsulates its purpose in this notion of love. He, more than any other first-century writer, with the exception of St. Paul, became the torchbearer of the essence of faith, which he elaborated in his Gospel and letters.

DISCIPLESHIP

Chosen to be disciples while fishing at Lake Galilee, John and his brother James were called "sons of thunder" by Jesus for their fiery temperament. Some believe this to be an allusion to their status as zealots, or freedom fighters, intent on raising rebellion against the Roman occupiers. More apparent is that he became one of an inner group, along with James and Peter, who were privileged witnesses to certain events, such as the raising of Jairus's daughter, the Transfiguration, and the Agony in the Garden of Gethsemane.

John is thought to be the mysterious "beloved disciple" of the Fourth Gospel, since he is not named in person elsewhere in the book. It is he who leaned against Christ's breast at the Last Supper, he whom Jesus charges with the care of his mother Mary at the foot of the cross, and he who ran with Peter to the tomb on the morning of the Resurrection.

LATER LIFE

There is some doubt about whether the apostle John was the same person as the evangelist who wrote the Fourth Gospel. If they are one and the same, he wrote it in Ephesus, one of the Greek-speaking colonies of Christians he founded in western Asia Minor (Turkey), and where he settled. By this time he was an old man living at the end of the first century. The city, as with most in the region, was a hotbed of pagan idolatry. One of the most popular gods was Diana, whose high priest, it is said, once challenged John to drink a poisoned cup, giving rise to his symbol in art of a viper in a cup.

While condemned by Emperor Domitian to exile on the island of Patmos, John received the vision of the Apocalypse, or Book of Revelation, which he addressed to his "seven churches of Asia."

St. John in the Isle of Patmos.

ABOVE *A 19th-century woodcut of St. John with his evangelist's emblem of the eagle.*

VALENTINE (DIED C. 261)

FEAST DAY: *February 14*
SYMBOLS IN ART: *Rosebush, birds, heart pierced by arrow*
PATRONAGE: *Lovers*
PAINTINGS: *Bassano, Jacopo*, St. Valentine Baptizing St. Lucilla
PROFILE: *Early Roman martyr who unwittingly gave rise to a festival of lovers*

ABOVE *There is much doubt about who the real St. Valentine was. He may have been the third-century bishop of Terni, seen here baptizing a new member into the faith, for which the priest sacrificed his life.*

THERE ARE TWO POSSIBLE FIGURES behind this name: One was a Roman priest and doctor who was martyred c. 261, the other was a bishop of Terni, also a martyr, whose relics were later transported to Rome. However, it is unlikely that either of these churchmen were responsible for the tradition on St. Valentine's Day of courting lovers. St. Valentine's Day as a lovers' festival dates at least to the fourteenth century. The medieval English writer Geoffrey Chaucer knew of it.

The idea that on this day people find their partner seems to be based on the belief that birds pair off on February fourteenth. A further possible basis for the tradition is the Roman Lupercalia festival, celebrated in mid-February, when partners were chosen by lot. This may also explain the tradition of anonymity that is associated with the modern custom of writing cards and messages of love unsigned.

Whatever the real historical background, there is no connection between ancient Roman martyrs and the huge commercial orgy of scent and sentiment that characterizes today's celebrations for expectant lovers around the world.

RIVAL RELIQUARIES

Since 1835 the Carmelite Whitefriar Street Church in Dublin has claimed to possess the relics of St. Valentine. But there is also a shrine to him at the Gorbals area of Glasgow in Scotland. The friars of St. Francis's Church say that St. Valentine's remains have been kept there in a wooden casket ever since 1868 when a French owner of various religious memorabilia handed them over to the friars for safe keeping.

While there is no way of establishing whether the Irish or the Scots are the true owners of the saints' bones, it is hoped in both camps that the real message of St. Valentine's Day will not be lost, namely that martyrdom is the highest form of love.

Helen (Helena) (c. 250–330)

FEAST DAY:	*August 18 (West), May 21 (East)*
SYMBOLS IN ART:	*Cross*
PATRONAGE:	*Divorcées, difficult marriages, archaeologists*
PAINTING:	*da Conegliano, Cima, St. Helena*
PROFILE:	*Mother of the first Christian emperor Constantine; journeyed to Jerusalem and, according to tradition, discovered the True Cross of Jesus*

THE DEED THAT MADE HELEN FAMOUS—finding the cross on which Jesus was crucified—is treated by historians with a good deal of skepticism. What is beyond reasonable doubt is that this plucky empress undertook a long pilgrimage to the Holy Land as an elderly woman and died devoting her energy to caring for the poor.

What is known of Helen's early life is uncertain. The medieval chronicler Geoffrey of Monmouth claimed she was daughter of the legendary British King Cole and was born in York. More likely is that she was born to an innkeeper of Bithynia in Asia Minor. She was spotted by the Roman general Constantius, who took her to be his wife—but only until he was promoted to the rank of caesar, when it was deemed politically expedient to divorce Helen and marry the stepdaughter of the emperor Maximian.

Their marriage had lasted some 20 years and from it came a son who became emperor Constantine the Great. His proclamation in 312 that Christianity should be "tolerated" in the empire also occasioned her conversion, at over 60 years of age. Using treasury funds, she spent her time promoting Christian values, building churches, and giving alms to prisoners and the poor. When her son also became master of the Eastern Empire in 324, Helen felt it was safe enough to fulfill her ambition of making the pilgrimage to the Holy Land in order to venerate the sacred places of Jesus's life.

THE TRUE CROSS

When Constantine converted to Christianity in 312, Jerusalem was no longer a Jewish city. A temple to the pagan goddess Venus stood on the site of Jesus's tomb on Mount Calvary. Constantine's instruction to have the site excavated and to build the Church of the Holy Sepulchre provided the pretext for Helen to visit Palestine at nearly 80 years of age. According to St. Ambrose—a story romanticized in Cynewulf's ninth-century poem *Elene*—Helen is credited with finding three crosses in a rock cistern. To ascertain on which one Christ was hung, a woman with an incurable disease was asked to touch each of the crosses in turn. Her instant recovery on touching one was regarded as a sign that it was the True Cross.

Helen's feast was observed in many English monasteries, especially in the northeast of the country, where her son Constantine was proclaimed caesar by his troops at York. The town of St. Helens in Lancashire owes its name to her churches built there.

BELOW *A Greek icon of St. Helen and her son Constantine the Great marks the reverence paid to both figures in the Eastern Orthodox tradition.*

BASIL THE GREAT (330–379)

FEAST DAY:	*January 2*
SYMBOLS IN ART:	*Book, dove, fire*
PATRONAGE:	*Eastern Orthodox monks*
PAINTINGS:	*Subleyras, Pierre*, Mass of St. Basil
PROFILE:	*Doctor of the Church; Bishop of Caesarea of Cappadocia, Turkey; philanthropist*

THE CAPPADOCIAN FATHERS

❖

Basil was one of a trio of theologians—the others being his younger brother, Gregory of Nyssa, and Gregory of Nazianzus—who were known as the Cappadocian Fathers, named after the region of eastern Asia Minor (now Turkey) where they lived. Their main contribution to Christian theology was establishing a formula for the thorny issue of the Holy Trinity. They asserted that God was one substance but three persons in the Father, the Son, and the Holy Spirit. Although accepted at the time by all, the matter would arise again later in the history of the Church and contribute to the Great Schism between East and West of 1054.

ABOVE *St. Basil of Caesarea.*

THE BISHOP OF CAESAREA (from 370) came from a highly educated, wealthy family which could boast six saints across three generations. His greatest achievement was probably the Rule he laid down for the monastic life of the Eastern Orthodox Church. The Rule still provides its basis today.

As well as devising a system for the ideal religious life, Basil was equally concerned with improving the lives of the poor. During a famine he set up a soup kitchen and served food to the hungry. He used a good deal more of his inheritance in financing the construction of virtually an entire new town, Basiliad. Streets of houses went up; a hospital for the sick and hostel for travelers were designed; and doctors, nurses, and artisans were all employed as permanent staff. He was a philanthropist who anticipated the ventures of some nineteenth-century industrialists, such as the Victorian Cadbury brothers, who built communities for their employees.

A CHURCH FOR ALL

Basil was keen to promote a faith that included as much as possible of what was good in society. The Church had to embrace the people, not distance itself from them—including wrongdoers. In the case of petty criminals, for example, he emphasized the need for reform rather than punishment, and he pressured judges into moderating their sentences. Basil's striving for social harmony was also expressed in his Rule for the religious life. Rather than individual ascetic practices, Basil encouraged activities to benefit the community as a whole, such as duties in hospitals and guest houses. He did not, however, neglect the value of the contemplative life. Perhaps it was his balance of the spiritual and the practical that made Basil's achievements so effective and lasting.

ABOVE *An early 19th-century Russian engraving shows St. Basil and St. Maximus the Monk in debate. Both theologians, who lived three centuries apart, were later championed for their defense of the faith against heresy.*

JOHN CHRYSOSTOM (347–407)

FEAST DAY:	*September 13 (West), November 13 (East)*
SYMBOLS IN ART:	*Byzantine church*
PATRONAGE:	*Preachers*
PAINTINGS:	*None known*
PROFILE:	*One of four Doctors of the Eastern Church of the Roman Empire; Archbishop of Constantinople*

ABOVE As Archbishop of Constantinople, John Chrysostom was he most authoritative figure in the Eastern Church. His gift for oratory also made him a great force in politics.

THE MAN WHO CHAMPIONED the cause of Christian ethics was aptly nicknamed Chrysostom, or "Golden Mouth," for the eloquence with which he spoke out against the decadence of society in his day.

This son of an army officer, who died when John was still a baby, lived with his mother until her death. Then he retired to the mountains at the age of 27 and lived in a cave community of hermits for six years until his health faltered. On returning to Antioch in Syria, he acquired a reputation for preaching—preaching that was simple and direct, using language that the ordinary person in the street could understand. The inner search for truth that had led him into religious retreat now compelled him to speak out against the misuse of power and wealth he saw around him. Perhaps some of his popular appeal was just that lack of compromise he showed when pointing the finger at high society.

MORAL CRUSADER

As Archbishop of Constantinople (from 398), John was invested with the highest church authority in Eastern Christendom. He was also ensconced in a cosmopolitan city with excessive lifestyles. He criticized laity and clergy alike for their fondness of luxury at the expense of those in need. Specifically, he targeted the women at court whose behavior, clothes, and makeup he regarded as vain and licentious. The spiteful empress Eudoxia took his attempts at reform as a personal attack and accused him of insulting her by calling her "Jezebel," after the Israelite queen of idolatry. Through a conspiracy involving the numerous enemies that John had now made in the Church, she had him deposed and sent into exile in 403.

An immediate earthquake worried her that she may have invoked God's wrath, and she begged the maverick cleric to return to Constantinople. He agreed, only to see before the great door of his beloved Cathedral of Hagia Sophia a troupe of licentious pagans cavorting around a silver statue of the empress. True to form, John Chrysostom vented an unbridled condemnation. The paranoid queen shuddered with indignation and ordered him to be banished indefinitely to Armenia. As his enemies pursued him eastward, hardship took its toll and he died of exhaustion.

SIMEON THE STYLITE (390–459)

FEAST DAY:	*January 5 (West), September 1 (East)*
SYMBOLS IN ART:	*Pillar*
PATRONAGE:	*None*
PAINTINGS:	*None known*
PROFILE:	*Hermit who lived on top of a pillar in Syria*

HERMITS DWELLING in caves had chosen austere enough lifestyles, but there were others who outdid them: The so-called stylites, who lived on top of pillars. The first and most famous example of this extreme brand of asceticism, common to Syria, was St. Simeon.

His call to a new life came in a vision he experienced while helping to lay the foundations of a new house. Its message, that he should dig deeper, he took to be a sign that he ought to retreat from society. As a result he gave up his usual occupation as a shepherd and joined a local monastery.

FEATS OF SPIRITUAL ENDURANCE

Simeon's life is a catalogue of ever-increasing levels of self-mortification. At one stage he nearly died after he had entwined himself in a rope of twisted palm leaves, which cut into his flesh. It took three days of surgical treatment to remove the vegetation. His first Lent was spent abstaining from all food and water, a fast that left him unconscious through weakness. A simple diet of holy bread and wine, together with some lettuce leaves, proved sufficient to revive him.

By the time he had conceived his next act—climbing to the top of a mountain and chaining himself to a rock within a deep-sided cave—word had got around about the extraordinary feats of self-denial this monk could endure. He proved an interesting and wise counselor to his curious visitors, and no matter how remote his refuge they sought him out.

VERTICAL TAKE-OFF

In a bid to distance himself more effectively, Simeon struck upon his famous innovation of erecting a pillar on which only he stood. At first it was low, then he increased the height until it reached nearly 65 feet (20 meters). A balustrade surrounded a platform at the top to keep him from falling when he slept. There he stayed for the last 36 years of his life, entirely dependent on others, who would hoist up food and water to him. It is said that "despairing of escaping the world horizontally, he escaped it vertically."

THE FIRST AGONY COLUMN

Alas this stunt only served to make the eccentric hermit more popular than ever. Crowds flocked from all parts of Europe to ask his advice. He became a sort of "agony uncle." His replies were always sympathetic. He preached daily, frequently against the twin evils of lust and luxury, and he found a large number of conversions among his listeners, especially Bedouin Arabs in the region.

Thus began a tradition that other ascetics emulated over the next 500 years. Alfred, Lord Tennyson wrote a poem about its founder, whose pillar base can still be seen at Qala' at Samaan.

ABOVE St. Simeon, Hermit of the Pillar, attracted crowds of onlookers as much for his charm and wisdom as for his chosen manner of isolation.

BENEDICT (C. 480–C. 547)

FEAST DAY:	*July 11*
SYMBOLS IN ART:	*Broken cup (containing poison), raven, Rule book*
PATRONAGE:	*Europe*
PAINTINGS:	*Perugino, Pietro*, St. Benedict; *Spinello, Aretino*, Stories from the Legend of St. Benedict *(fresco)*
PROFILE:	*Abbot at Monte Cassino (Italy) and Father of Western monasticism*

UNTIL THE SIXTH CENTURY, monks in Western Europe tended to lead austere lives, often as isolated hermits. At first Benedict was no different. Born into a wealthy family in Nursia in Italy, he studied in Rome before the profligacy of urban life drove him to seek solitude in a cave. It was so remote that food had to be lowered to him on a rope; his only companion was a raven. He acquired a reputation as a holy man and in time was asked to help with the organization of monks into religious communities. The result was the founding of his famous monastery at Monte Cassino, plus 12 other monasteries in the region. In these institutions he implemented his supreme Rule for the monastic life, which eventually became the standard throughout Western Christendom.

What Benedict created was an extension of his own character: Prudence and moderation set within a framework of discipline. Although he borrowed elements from other more austere traditions, Benedict's achievement lay in his ability to create a workable organization flexible enough to adapt to the needs of different societies. Many monasteries later became centers for different purposes, such as for hospitality, medicine, agriculture, or learning.

Benedict's system was far removed from earlier models of the spiritual life. Gone were the harsh strictures of the zealot in the desert. Instead there was emphasis on collective prayer and manual work conducted in a gentler mood more suited to Europe. As Benedictine monasticism spread across the continent in the coming centuries, it was his values of the religious life that gave Europe a sense of identity and unity, and for this reason Pope Paul VI made St. Benedict its patron in 1964.

AN ORDER OF MODERATION AND MUTUAL HELP

St. Benedict ruled that:

- A monastery should, if possible, be built so that everything needed—that is, water, mill, garden, bakery—may be available.
- A mattress, woolen blanket, woolen underblanket, and a pillow shall suffice for bedding.
- When the brothers rise for the service of God, they should gently encourage one another, because the sleepy ones are apt to make excuses.
- The brothers shall take turns waiting on each other so that no one is excused from kitchen work.
- There shall be complete silence at the table. The brethren should pass to each other in turn whatever food is needed so that no one need ask for anything.
- We read that wine is not suitable for monks. But because, in our day, it is not possible to persuade monks of this, let us agree at least that we should not drink to excess. We believe that one pint of wine a day is enough.

See also ANTONY *page 22,* BASIL THE GREAT *page 46*

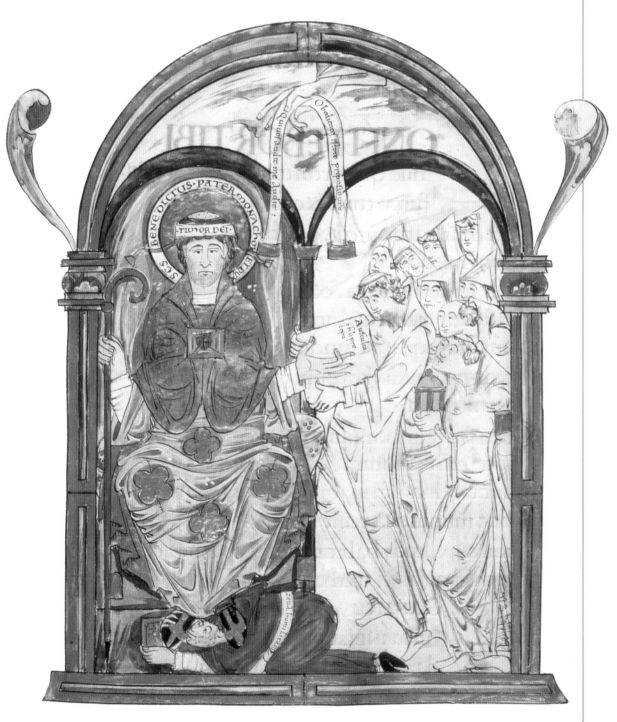

ABOVE *In an 11th-century miniature, monks from Canterbury pay homage to St. Benedict, founder of a way of monastic life that came to dominate Western medieval society.*

BEDE LEVENERABLE

ABOVE *A 16th-century woodcut exhibits all the trappings of the erudite monk from Jarrow, Northumberland: Writing slope, quill pen, inkwell, scissors, and candle, for long hours of painstaking scholarship.*

THE VENERABLE BEDE (673–735)

FEAST DAY:	*May 25*
SYMBOLS IN ART:	*Book, pen, monk at a desk*
PATRONAGE:	*None*
PAINTINGS:	*None known*
PROFILE:	*Monk, biblical scholar, first English historian,*
	Doctor of the Church

THE HOMELY MONK from Jarrow, a small town in the Anglo-Saxon kingdom of Northumbria, is considered to have been the best known and perhaps most influential writer in Western Europe from the eighth to the twelfth centuries. His prolific writing and breadth of knowledge provided a lone beacon for future historians of the Dark Ages. His most valuable work, *Ecclesiastical History of the English People,* is one of the world's great historical works, a rich tapestry of information woven together from a myriad sources. He also took the trouble, unusual for his day, of differentiating between fact and hearsay. He compiled the first martyrology of saints' lives and expounded on other unrelated subjects, such as science and grammar. Although most of his works were penned in Latin, he was the first known writer of English prose.

Wide though his compass of scholarship was, in his lifetime Bede probably never ventured beyond Northumbria. In the monk's own words, "I have devoted my energies to the study of the scriptures, observing monastic discipline, and singing the daily services in church; study, teaching and writing have always been my delight."* From the early age of seven he was educated at local monasteries. At Jarrow he became a monk and priest before spending the rest of his life there.

Bede wrote *Ecclesiastical History* at a time when Christianity was still a relatively new faith to the mixed Anglo-Saxons of Britain, and he portrays it as a unifying force. He is conscious of the debt owed to Irish monks, such as Columba and Aidan, who imported their Celtic brand of the faith, and he fondly contrasts their holiness with the slothfulness of his compatriots. Bede's personal qualities of humility and precision are apparent in the work—so too are his prejudices: He clearly preferred orthodox Roman liturgy to any traditions of the Celtic Church. His histories were the first known to use *Anno Domini* (A.D.) in dating.

The title of "Venerable," meaning worthy of honor, was given to Bede by a ninth-century synod. It was not until 1899 that he was recognized as a Doctor of the Church by Pope Leo XIII. He is the only Englishman named by Dante in his poetic work *Paradiso.*

ABOVE *An historian of distinction, Bede was one of the few writers of his time to take the trouble to differentiate between fact and hearsay.*

*D. Attwater, *Penguin Dictionary of Saints*

See also COLUMBA *page 34*

ANSELM (1033–1109)

FEAST DAY:	*April 21*
SYMBOLS IN ART:	*Ship*
PATRONAGE:	*None*
PAINTINGS:	*None known*
PROFILE:	*"Father of Scholasticism," Archbishop of Canterbury; fierce opponent of the slave trade*

So HIGHLY REGARDED was this martyr for the faith that the medieval poet Dante depicted Anselm as one of the spirits of light and power in his work, *Paradiso*. Though he was an intellectual ranked alongside Saints Augustine and Aquinas, his gentleness of spirit and love for his flock made him a popular figure with the people of his time. He adopted an uncompromising stance toward injustice in society. He was a fierce opponent of slavery—one of his secular achievements was the introduction of legislation in England prohibiting the sale of men.

Anselm's introduction to ecclesiastical office in England came by way of appointment to the archbishopric of Canterbury in 1093. Born of Italian nobility, he was used to the unquestioned supremacy of the pope in any religious matters. So arriving to find that William II (Rufus) of England was intent on throwing his weight around in the appointment of bishops took him by surprise. Despite his quiet nature, Anselm could be obstinate whenever he felt the Church's authority was undermined. His refusal to compromise over the issue of episcopal succession brought him into constant conflict with the state and several times he was forced to leave the country for his own safety. This may explain his symbol in art as a ship.

PHILOSOPHER OF GOD

Much of his philosophical theology was worked out in exile. As one of the early medieval Scholastics, who based their methods on those of the Latin Fathers and Aristotle, Anselm shone like a beacon among theologians of his time in Europe. Unlike his contemporaries, he defended the Christian faith by intellectual reasoning rather than by arguments based on Scripture and other authorities. He outlined the systematic reasoning for the existence of God known as the "ontological proof," in which he argued that the mere existence of the *idea* that there is a God necessarily involves the objective existence of God. He always said that he did not seek first to understand in order to believe in God, but rather that unless he believed he would not understand. His "faith seeking understanding" has become a popular maxim in the Church.

ABOVE *The novel approach of philosopher St. Anselm to his Christian faith was to defend it by reason, unlike his contemporaries who made Scripture their authority.*

FRANCES OF ROME (1384–1440)

FEAST DAY:	*March 9*
SYMBOLS IN ART:	*Woman dressed in black with white veil accompanied by an angel*
PATRONAGE:	*Motorists, taxi drivers, death of children, widows*
PAINTINGS:	*Gentileschi, Orazio, The Vision of St. Francesca Romana*
PROFILE:	*Wife, mother, and mystic; founder of a society of pious women*

THERE ARE MANY EXAMPLES of holy women who have turned their backs on the world by taking vows, selling their property, and retreating into a cloister. St. Frances of Rome was devout but did none of these things—she stayed firmly "in the world."

Born into an aristocratic family, she was married against her wishes at the age of thirteen. Fortunately, the marriage was a happy one, without ever a quarrel, it is said, in its 40 years. They had possibly as many as six children, of whom two died while still young.

Frances had a strong sympathy for the sufferings of others, and during epidemics of plague and civil war she tended to the sick. The more acts of charity she performed the more value she saw in a life of self-denial and service to the community. Together with other women in Rome she set up a society in 1425 in aid of the poor and distressed, and later founded a community known as the Oblates of Mary.

GUARDIAN ANGELS

Frances was one of the greatest mystics of the fifteenth century. On the anniversary of the death of her son Evangelista, aged nine, she received a vision of an angel in company with him. A brilliant light at dawn filled her oratory for an hour during which Evangelista revealed that God was sending her this archangel, who would remain with her day and night. Her son then disappeared, never to be seen again.

Thereafter, Frances said the archangel enveloped her in a halo of light, though no one else was able to see it. She was apparently able to see in the dark by a light illuminating her path ahead, a phenomenon thought to explain her patronage of motorists. She described the archangel as a sweetly spoken boy of nine with hair like spun gold. The archangel, who gave no name, stayed by her side for 26 years, counseling and enabling her to perceive the thoughts of others. She was reported to have used this supernatural blessing to detect plots of ill intent, but by the same token it made her uncomfortably aware of evil in the world. She became dependent on the archangel for protection, especially when her husband was forced into exile.

When her husband died, Frances joined her own community and experienced another vision, this time of God seated on a high throne surrounded by angels. One of the angelic "powers" replaced the archangel as Frances's protector for the last four years of her life. He is said to have carried three palm branches in his left hand, symbolizing the virtues of charity, firmness, and prudence, which he would help Frances to cultivate.

ABOVE *St. Frances, portrayed with the Madonna and child, claimed to see angels after the death of her son.*

THOMAS MORE (1478–1535)

FEAST DAY:	*June 22*
SYMBOLS IN ART:	*None*
PATRONAGE:	*Civil servants, politicians, large families, difficult marriages*
PAINTINGS:	*Holbein the Younger, Hans,* Portrait of Sir Thomas More; *Caron, Antoine,* Arrest and Execution of Thomas More
PROFILE:	*English statesman, humanist, and martyr*

UTOPIAN SOCIETY

❖

Coined from the Greek, meaning "no place" and "good place," More's famous work, *Utopia*, describes an ideal community living in harmony. It revolutionized the Greek philosopher Plato's classical model of the perfect republic, mainly by proposing realistic aims. Thomas More set his island community in the recently discovered New World and contrasted its life with the corruption and inequality evident in his own day. In his imaginary world there is religious toleration for all, equal education for boys and girls, a set length to the work day, and no private property. The book was a bestseller when first published in 1516, and was later thought to be used by Anabaptists, Mormons, and even communists.

LIVING IN AN AGE when political corruption was rife, Thomas More became a beacon of moral courage. His resolute commitment to the principles of his faith when challenged so persistently by Henry VIII over his divorce led him to pay the ultimate price of sacrificing his life.

Formerly, the two men had been friends. During the 1520s the king would sail down the River Thames to visit More in Chelsea, usually to ask his advice on how best to divorce Catherine of Aragon. Having a reputation for fairness and integrity as

ABOVE *St. Thomas More as Lord Chancellor. Portrait by Holbein.*

a judge, More succeeded Cardinal Wolsey as Lord Chancellor in 1529. He led a cultured life debating matters with such friends as the humanists Erasmus and Colet. In educating his daughters, he was progressive for his day, but devotion to God took precedence over all. Evenings were spent solemnly with his family reading passages from Scripture and saying prayers together.

RUPTURE WITH THE KING

Little by little the friendship with Henry deteriorated. The king was determined to declare his marriage to Catherine of Aragon invalid so that he could marry Anne Boleyn. His insistence that the clergy acknowledge him as supreme head of the Church of England—in other words, higher in authority than the pope—was unacceptable to More, and he resigned as Lord Chancellor.

Relations were now bad enough but the real crisis came in 1534 with the Act of Succession. Despite the pope's verdict that Henry's union with Catherine was still valid, the king went ahead and married Anne. Not only did he require his subjects to accept their children as legitimate heirs to the throne, but he also demanded recognition that his earlier marriage to Catherine was not valid. More's refusal to do this rendered him guilty of high treason. He was imprisoned in the Tower of London, where he spent the next 15 months. His lands were confiscated and his family was forced into poverty. At a show trial in Westminster Hall he was sentenced to death by beheading. His canonization took place in 1935.

ABOVE The Arrest and Execution of Thomas More *by Antoine Caron
(1515–1593). As the martyr is led to the gallows, he is followed on horseback
by soldiers and King Henry VIII, in red, emerging from the archway.*

IGNATIUS LOYOLA (1491–1556)

FEAST DAY:	*July 31*
SYMBOLS IN ART:	*None*
PATRONAGE:	*Spiritual exercises and retreats, soldiers, certain schools and colleges*
PAINTINGS:	*Montanez, Juan Martinez*, St. Ignatius Loyola; *de Rocalde, Inigo Lopez*, St. Ignatius Loyola; *Rubens, Peter Paul*, The Miracles of St. Ignatius of Loyola
PROFILE:	*Founder of the Society of Jesus (Jesuits)*

A NOBLEMAN FROM THE BASQUE COUNTRY spearheaded the Roman Catholic Counter-Reformation movement of the sixteenth century through his foundation of the missionary religious order, the Society of Jesus, or Jesuits.

Ignatius, from Loyola in northern Spain, was a soldier and might have followed the example of his compatriots as a buccaneering conquistador to the New World had he not had his leg shattered by a cannonball during a campaign against the French. During his convalescence he looked around for his preferred reading matter of romantic adventures, only to find the Bible and a collection of saints' lives. These seemed to have inspired a change in outlook, for when he recovered, albeit with a permanent limp, he applied all the discipline and obedience of his military training to becoming a soldier of Christ in emulation of the heroic lives of the saints: "St. Dominic did this, therefore I must do it. St. Francis did this, therefore I must do it."*

During a year spent in retreat Ignatius wrote a spiritual manual, *Spiritual Exercises*, which he used while a student in Paris to initiate a small circle of followers, including Francis Xavier, future Jesuit missionary to the Far East. The group vowed to dedicate their lives to Christ and to the instruction of children and the uneducated. They offered complete obedience to the pope, promising to take the Gospel to anywhere he directed, even to Protestants. This was a welcome initiative at a time when the Roman Catholic Church had lost great numbers of its believers to breakaway Protestant churches—and much revenue with it. A grateful Pope Paul III endorsed the Society of Jesus in 1540 with Ignatius as its first general, a position he held until his death.

The Jesuits quickly established a reputation for effective missionary and educational work. By the time of Ignatius's death, there were more than 1,000 Jesuits operating in Europe and as far away as Brazil and China.

SPIRITUAL EXERCISES

❖

The manual written by Ignatius was a four-week program designed as a sort of spiritual assault course for new soldiers of Jesus. Week-on-week meditations proceeded through sin, the kingship of Christ, his Passion, and finally his risen life. Its militaristic tone even includes a progress chart by which individuals can assess their performance. The self-discipline that was guaranteed to be beneficial had a certain appeal, in the way that yoga has today, though some of its language betrayed a medieval-like obsession with self-loathing and the terrors of damnation.

*Ignatius, *Autobiography*

See also FRANCIS XAVIER *page 82*

ABOVE *The man who started out in life as a Spanish soldier taught a higher form of loyalty in his missionary Society of Jesus (Jesuits). Oil painting by Rubens.*

Martin de Porres (1579–1639)

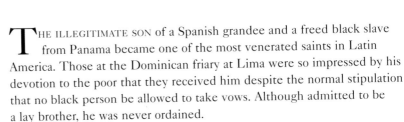

FEAST DAY:	*November 3*
SYMBOLS IN ART:	*None*
PATRONAGE:	*Racial harmony and social justice, hairdressers*
PAINTINGS:	*None known*
PROFILE:	*Dominican friar from Lima, Peru; first black American saint*

T HE ILLEGITIMATE SON of a Spanish grandee and a freed black slave from Panama became one of the most venerated saints in Latin America. Those at the Dominican friary at Lima were so impressed by his devotion to the poor that they received him despite the normal stipulation that no black person be allowed to take vows. Although admitted to be a lay brother, he was never ordained.

Martin was apprenticed to a barber and surgeon, from whom he learned about medicine and care of the sick. He established an orphanage and a children's hospital for the poor tenants in the slums.

ABOVE *The first black American saint, canonized in 1962, came to the fore as a symbol of racial harmony when the black civil rights movement in the U.S. peaked.*

As well as working at the monastery as a gardener and barber, he spent his days tending to the sick and the poor, irrespective of their ethnicity and color. His nights were spent in prayer and penitence, and he sometimes experienced visions and religious ecstasy. He fasted frequently and never ate meat.

His reputation for holiness grew to the extent that people started seeking him out for spiritual advice. After he successfully solved his sister's marital problems, the influential citizens of Lima came for counseling on more delicate matters of the heart, too.

When he died of a fever at the age of 60, all of Lima acclaimed his holiness and his body was borne to the grave by prelates and noblemen. Several miraculous cures are said to have occurred at his tomb as well as during his lifetime, and the beatification process began in 1660. However, not until 1962 was he finally canonized by Pope John XXIII. In the United States, Martin has been adopted as patron saint of racial harmony, not through any political activity, but for his caring charity to people of all ethnic backgrounds.

TIRELESS WORKER

Martin became known as the "father of charity" for his dedication to others. He bought a Negro slave his freedom, employing him to work in the laundry, and with him looked after those in need of blankets and clothes. He distributed the monastery's alms to the poor, purportedly increasing it miraculously. He even demonstrated how to sow chamomile into the hoof prints of cattle. A love of animals resulted in his building a shelter for stray cats and dogs, of which the sick ones he would nurse back to health.

VINCENT DE PAUL (C. 1581–1660)

FEAST DAY:	*September 27*
SYMBOLS IN ART:	*None*
PATRONAGE:	*Charities*
PAINTINGS:	*None known*
PROFILE:	*French founder of charitable orders*

AFTER THE RELIGIOUS upheaval of the Reformation, a spirit of renewal led some individuals to anticipate the Age of Enlightenment by encouraging such ideals as the equality of men and women. Foremost among them was the French priest Vincent de Paul, whose selfless devotion to all made him a legend in his own lifetime.

LEFT *Vincent de Paul, French priest and philanthropist whose heart went out to every man, woman, and child in need.*

The early years spent as a priest in a comfortable rural parish in Gascony were no preparation for a series of events that would change his life. Having enjoyed society life in Paris as a tutor to a count's family, Vincent is said to have been captured by Turkish pirates and enslaved for two years in Tunisia before escaping. He endured terrible conditions and his encounters with convicts, galley slaves, street urchins, and the destitute opened his eyes to everyday suffering that he had not known existed, let alone experienced.

He dedicated the rest of his life to relieving the suffering of mankind, and also to teaching and preaching, so that such ignorance among the clergy, as he had been guilty of, should be reduced as much as possible.

FOUNDATION OF NURSES

His humility and sensitivity engendered a like spirit in others, especially among women. In setting up the Sisters of Charity with Louise de Marillac, Vincent created the first house of nuns not confined to an enclosure, who were devoted to caring for the poor and the sick. Women worked closely with their neighbors on local needs, and the institution became famous throughout Europe for its nursing care. Even Florence Nightingale, a Protestant, was said to have been greatly influenced by the sisters of St. Vincent de Paul in her ministry to the victims of the Crimean War in the nineteenth century.

POWER OF THE MEDIA

Before broadcast was possible through newspapers and other mass media, the main voice on matters of public concern was the church sermon. This was no more apparent than in the age of Louis XIV, when the pulpit was commonly used for political ends in shaping public opinion. Vincent de Paul was horrified at such abuse of power and spoke out vehemently against it, preaching instead on how energy and resources could be well directed in relieving the plight of the poor. His Order of Lazarites was founded in 1625 partly to encourage a social conscience among the rural clergy.

See also LOUISE DE MARILLAC *page 150*

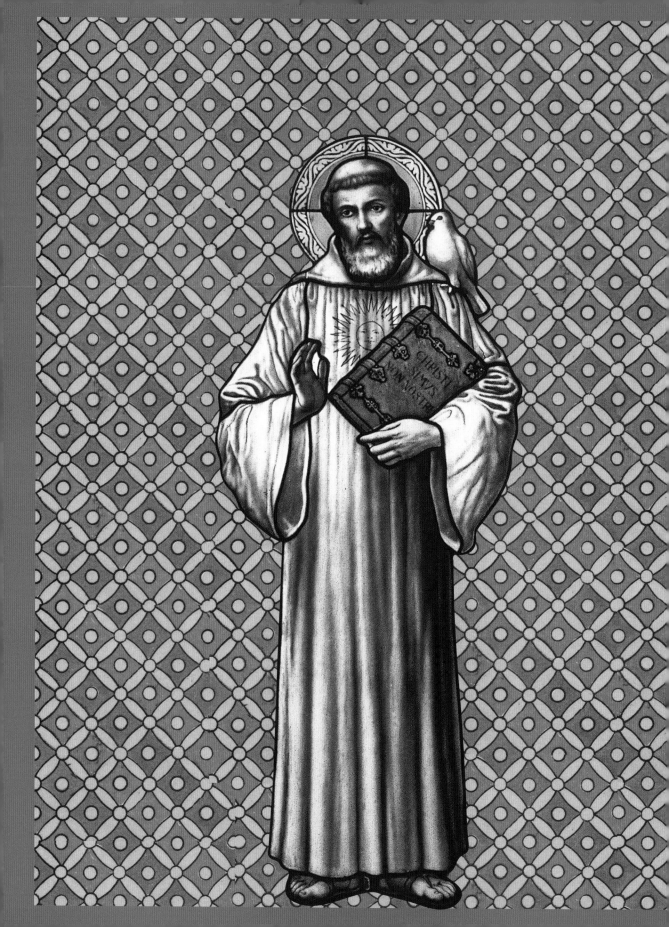

CHAPTER 4

MISSION
AND
TRAVEL

JAMES "THE GREATER" (DIED 44)

FEAST DAY:	*July 25*
SYMBOLS IN ART:	*Pilgrim's hat and staff, scallop shell, key, sword*
PATRONAGE:	*Spain, Chile, pilgrims, rheumatism, arthritis, horsemen, soldiers*
PAINTINGS:	*El Greco,* St. James the Great; *Cano, Alonso,* St. James the Greater; *Rubens,* St. James the Apostle; *Poussin, Nicolas,* The Virgin Appearing to St. James the Great
PROFILE:	*Fisherman and first apostle of Jesus to be martyred; by tradition, the founder of the Church in Spain, with relics held at Santiago de Compostela*

MEDIEVAL PILGRIMAGE

❖

In an age obsessed with death and the consequences of sin, the only way to avoid the coming torments of Hell was to do penance for one's sins while still on Earth. One of the more pleasant ways of doing it was to go on pilgrimage, the tourism of the Middle Ages. As with a package tour today, organized groups of pilgrims—some serious in sackcloth and bare of foot, others lighter in heart—would set out along established routes visiting one shrine after another and end up at some glorious destination such as Jerusalem, Rome, or Santiago de Compostela. Pilgrims venerated the relics of saints, believing them to have the power to absolve their sins and even effect miraculous cures.

WHILE MENDING FISHING NETS with his brother John the Evangelist and his father Zebedee, James was picked out by Jesus to be his disciple. The two brothers were nicknamed "sons of thunder" for their fiery temperament, and they joined Peter in forming an inner circle of disciples who were witnesses to special events in Jesus's ministry. These included the raising of Jairus's daughter, the Transfiguration of Jesus on Mount Hermon, and the Agony in the Garden of Gethsemane at the beginning of Jesus's Passion.

Although there is no written record of James's travels after Christ's Ascension, tradition asserts that he underwent a missionary journey to Spain. However, the earliest reference to this comes in the seventh century, long after most of the country had become Christian. What is certain is that James was back in Palestine by 43 and was martyred in Jerusalem the following year by King Herod Agrippa I, who ordered a persecution of Christians to satisfy the Jews.

THE CULT OF SANTIAGO

His relics are said to have been taken to Spain, and eventually they formed the foundation of the medieval pilgrimage shrine at Santiago de Compostela ("Sant Iago" meaning Saint James) c. 840. During the wars with Moorish invaders from North Africa, St. James was adopted as a symbol of Christian defense against the infidel and he became patron of Spain. His cult grew to such an extent that his shrine at Compostela was among the most popular in medieval Christendom.

A string of Cluniac and Augustinian monasteries sprang up along the various routes through Europe to his shrine, providing hospitality for the thousands of pilgrims making the journey. The conquistadors took his cult to the New World and St. James was made patron saint of Chile, whose capital Santiago is named after him.

See also JOHN THE APOSTLE *page 42,* PETER *page 110*

ABOVE *St. James the Apostle was adopted as a symbol of Christian defense against the infidel in Spain. His horse bears the insignia of the scallop shell associated with his town of Compostela.*

PAUL (DIED C. 65)

FEAST DAY:	*June 29*
SYMBOLS IN ART:	*Sword, book, three springs of water*
PATRONAGE:	*Public relations personnel, rope makers, saddlers, sandal makers, writers, Rome, Greece; protector against snakes, hailstorms*
PAINTINGS:	*El Greco,* Apostle St. Paul*; Caravaggio,* The Conversion of St. Paul*; Beccafumi, Domenico,* St. Paul*; Rembrandt,* Apostle Paul*; Raffaello, Sanzio,* The Liberation of St. Peter *(fresco)*
PROFILE:	*Apostle to the Gentiles and co-founder of the Church with St. Peter*

ABOVE The conversion of St. Paul on the road to Damascus, from a 19th-century wood engraving.

MORE THAN ANY OTHER SAINT, Paul was responsible for shaping hChristianity. In his letters, which predate the Gospels, and the Acts of the Apostles, a corpus of belief emerged as the foundation for Christian thinking, especially on Jesus's divinity and Resurrection. It was Paul who understood Jesus's death as a divine sacrifice for the redemption of mankind, by which sin and death no longer held power over humanity.

SAUL—PERSECUTOR OF THE "NAZARENES"
Before Paul converted to Christ, he was a fierce opponent of the radical sect, whom the Jews called the "Nazarenes" after their leader, Jesus of Nazareth. As an influential Pharisee, Paul (whose Jewish name was Saul) used his authority to persecute Christians, including their first martyr St. Stephen.

It was during his journey to Damascus, to seek out and arrest more Christians, that he suffered a blinding conversion experience of Christ. Baptized in Damascus two days later, Paul was a changed man who devoted the rest of his life to spreading the Christian Gospel and expounding his conviction that Jesus was the long-awaited Messiah of Jewish belief.

MISSIONARY JOURNEYS
Paul had to flee from persecution himself when fellow Jews later discovered what he was doing; he retreated to his home town of Tarsus in Asia Minor (modern Turkey), where he worked as a tent maker. Safely away from the troublesome environment of Jerusalem, he spent much of his time evangelizing Jewish and Gentile communities in Asia Minor and Greece. He undertook three missionary journeys from 46 to 57 C.E., including a two-year stop at Ephesus, where he endeavored to overturn the pagan culture associated with the goddess Diana. He debated with philosophers at Athens, and through his Epistles ironed out theological problems arising in his fledgling churches, such as at Corinth and Ephesus and those of Galatia.

IMPRISONMENT IN ROME
When Paul returned to face the music in Jerusalem his enemies provoked a riot in the temple area, which resulted in his arrest and trial in Caesarea (the provincial capital) before the Roman authorities. As a Roman citizen, Paul was entitled to have his case heard by the emperor himself, and duly he undertook the voyage to Rome in order to clear his name. He was held under house arrest for two years. Tradition holds that he was put to death with St. Peter as scapegoats for the Great Fire of Rome in 64 C.E.

ABOVE *Raphael's representation of St. Paul in prison offering benediction to his oppressors.*

THOMAS THE APOSTLE (FIRST CENTURY)

FEAST DAY:	*July 3 (West); October 6 (East)*
SYMBOLS IN ART:	*Builder's T-square, belt, spear, dagger*
PATRONAGE:	*Protector against blindness; architects*
PAINTINGS:	*Guercino*, Doubting Thomas; *da Conegliano, Cima*, Incredulity of St. Thomas; *Rembrandt*, Incredulity of St. Thomas; *El Greco*, St. Thomas
PROFILE:	*Apostle and martyr; also known as "Doubting" Thomas and Didymus (meaning "twin"); tradition of mission to India*

ABOVE *Christ guides the hand of Doubting Thomas to his wounds in a 16th-century Flemish painting.*

O F THE OCCASIONS when Jesus appeared to his followers after his Resurrection, none is as human as the tale of Thomas. His doubt that Jesus had truly risen from the dead expresses a natural skepticism endearing to all who struggle with the faith. Although demanding of proof, Thomas became wholehearted in his belief once Christ's divinity was made plain to him.

MISSION TO INDIA?

According to tradition, Thomas took the Gospel to the Malabar coast in southwest India, a voyage well within the capability of seamen of the time. There still exists in that part an ancient community who call themselves "St. Thomas Christians."

Key moments in the saint's life, including the tale of how he came to be in India, are recounted in a third-century romance, called *The Acts of Thomas*. It tells of how Thomas was unwilling to take up his apostolic charge to go to India on the grounds that he could not make himself understood. However, while in Jerusalem, he was sold as a slave to an Indian merchant who was looking for a skilled carpenter. Thomas, a carpenter, was then taken to India and commissioned to build a palace for a king (hence his patronage of architects and his symbol in art of a builder's T-square).

The apostle decided to build not a physical palace but a spiritual one in Heaven by spending all his budget on the poor and the sick, whom he saw everywhere around him. When his master demanded to see the palace, Thomas explained, "Thou canst not see it now, but when thou departest this life then shalt thou see it." He was sent to jail. Further exploits led to his downfall and he was martyred with a spear near Madras.

Virtually nothing was known of the Thomas Christians until the Portuguese discovered them in 1500. Their language was Syriac, an ancient Syrian tongue close in style and vocabulary to Aramaic, which was spoken by Jesus and some of his followers. Although in every other way the church had been assimilated into Indian culture, their language and liturgy kept them apart from the ocean of Hinduism surrounding them.

Other writings accredited to St. Thomas are his apocryphal Gospel, consisting of sayings and parables of Jesus; his Gospel of Infancy, which records miracles supposedly performed by Christ as a child; and his Apocalypse, written pseudonymously in the fourth century.

His feast day is celebrated by employers who buy their staff seasonal drinks, a tradition known as "Thomasing."

MARK THE EVANGELIST (FIRST CENTURY)

FEAST DAY: *April 25*

SYMBOLS IN ART: *Winged lion*

PATRONAGE: *Venice*

PAINTINGS: *de Boulogne, Valentine*, St. Mark the Evangelist; *Tintoretto*, The Miracle of St. Mark Freeing the Slave, The Stealing of the Dead Body of Mark

PROFILE: *Author of the Gospel According to Mark; usually identified with John Mark of the Acts of the Apostles*

THERE IS SOME DOUBT about the authorship of St. Mark's gospel.

The writer was probably John Mark, who accompanied his cousin St. Barnabas and St. Paul on their first missionary journey outside Palestine. He also traveled with his cousin on a later missionary tour to Cyprus.

If the identification with John Mark is true, then his mother's house was a meeting place for apostles in Jerusalem. Early church fathers refer to him as the "mouthpiece," or interpreter, of the apostle Peter, and, according to St. Paul's Epistles, a Christian by the name of Mark was with Peter and Paul in Rome. It is likely that this person was the author of the Gospel.

ABOVE St. Mark the Evangelist *by Valentine de Boulogne (1591–1632)*.

THE "MARTYR'S GOSPEL"

As a companion of Peter, Mark would have been very familiar with the stories about Jesus, his teachings and parables, recounted numerous times during services and evangelizing missions. When Peter fell victim, as seems likely, to the persecution of Emperor Nero after the fire of Rome in 64 C.E., Mark felt it necessary to commit the collection of memoirs to paper.

The work was arranged with a theological purpose in mind. The early Church expected the present world soon to come to an end, when their savior would return, triumphant over the forces of evil, and bring in a new world order. But eyewitnesses to Jesus's ministry were dying off and Christians were often unpopular with the authorities, even suffering persecution for their beliefs. Reassurance was needed. Mark produced, in common Greek, a kind of religious pamphlet, which has been dubbed the "Martyr's Gospel," to be distributed to Roman Christians and other fledgling churches of the empire as a source of encouragement in hard times.

PATRON SAINT OF VENICE

Early tradition had it that St. Mark died in Alexandria. In a bold act of piracy, Venetian merchants of the ninth century smuggled his bones out of Egypt by hiding them in a barrel of salted pork, a place unlikely to be searched by Muslim officials. The relics now lie enshrined in St. Mark's Cathedral.

See also PAUL *page 66,* PETER *page 110*

CHRISTOPHER (THIRD CENTURY)

FEAST DAY:	*July 25 (formerly)*
SYMBOLS IN ART:	*Carrying infant Jesus, hermit, river, flowering staff, boats, fishes, temptresses, mermaid*
PATRONAGE:	*Travelers, especially motorists; protector against water, storm, plague, and sudden death*
PAINTINGS:	*Bellini, Giovanni*, St. Christopher; *Bouts, Dieric the Younger*, St. Christopher; *Patenier, Joachim*, St. Christopher Bearing the Christ Child; *Ribera, Jusepe de*, St. Christopher
PROFILE:	*Legendary martyr; one of the Fourteen Holy Helpers; reduced cult status in 1969*

PATRON OF TRAVELERS

❖

It was popularly believed that whoever set eyes on an image of St. Christopher would not die that day. In modern times he is invoked by travelers, especially motorists, before setting out on a journey. Their plaques often bear the inscription "Behold St. Christopher and go thy way in safety." As traveling on roadways and by air is perceived to have become more dangerous, so his cult has flourished. When the pope reduced him to local status (i.e., worthy only of local, not universal, veneration) in 1969, an outcry from many of his followers, led conspicuously by Italian film stars, showed just how strong the cult remained.

RIGHT *The saint honored by those whose burden feels heavy.*

ALL THAT IS KNOWN OF CHRISTOPHER is his martyrdom in Asia Minor (modern Turkey). Legend holds that he was a fearsome giant from Palestine whose wish was to serve the most powerful master in the world. He worshipped the devil for a time but discovered that he was afraid of a being named Jesus. While continuing his search, Christopher came upon a hermit who advised him to take up residence beside a river and put his strength to good use by helping travelers to cross it.

On one occasion a mysterious child asked for his assistance. Although little, the boy proved to be so heavy that Christopher bowed under his weight in midstream. Struggling against the torrent, Christopher cried out in frustration that he felt he was carrying the whole world. "You are," said the boy, "and him who made it." Only then did Christopher (whose name means "bearer of Christ") realize that he was carrying the Christ child on his shoulders.

MORE LEGEND

During the revelation Christopher was told to plant his staff in the ground; the next day it sprouted flowers and dates as a sign of the truth of the message he had received.

During a persecution of Christians (possibly that of Emperor Decius in 250), Christopher was imprisoned for refusing to worship the emperor. Tradition has it that two women sent to seduce him there were converted instead. Later he was beaten with iron rods and shot with arrows. Apparently surviving these punishments, the saint was finished off with decapitation.

S. CHRISTOPHE.

Heiliger Christoph.

Brendan the Navigator (c. 486–c. 575)

FEAST DAY:	*May 16*
SYMBOLS IN ART:	*Celebrating Mass on board a ship, sailing boat, whale*
PATRONAGE:	*Boatmen, sailors, travelers, whales, County Kerry in Ireland*
PAINTINGS:	*None known*
PROFILE:	*Abbot and pioneer of Irish monastic seafaring; his legend tells of a voyage around the north Atlantic Ocean. Also known as Brendan of Clonfert*

LIKE MANY OF THE IRISH MONKS, Brendan went on sea pilgrimages to spread the Christian faith. Having founded several monasteries in Ireland, including Clonfert (c. 560), he is said to have visited Columba in Scotland, founded an abbey in Wales, and ventured as far as Brittany with a companion saint whose name was given to the town that arose there, St. Malo. These journeys may not sound particularly adventurous by today's standards, but then the vessel they used was not one of today's choice, either: A 32-foot (9.7-meter) boat made of leather. Stretched over a wicker frame, the skin was kept waterproof by being greased with tallow and cod oil.

Few details about his life are known with certainty, but his cult flourished in Ireland from the ninth century, mainly on the strength of a mythical expedition he undertook to the "Land Promised to the Saints."

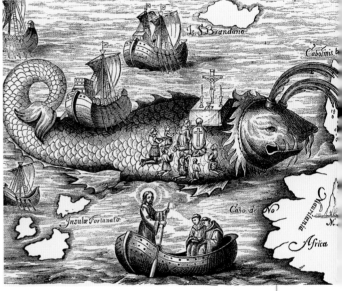

ABOVE *Brendan's mythical quest for the "Land of Saints" involved landing on a great fish in the Atlantic Ocean.*

DISCOVERER OF AMERICA?

A visionary romance, called the *Navigation of St. Brendan* (written c. 900), tells of the monk's quest for an earthly Paradise, when he sailed westward with 17 companions. Although the story is fictitious, many of its details point to known geographical facts. Directions and distances between lands visited are familiar to us—even their notes about the climate reflect true conditions. According to descriptions, the voyagers visit Rockall (an islet off Scotland), the Faeroe Islands, Iceland, and Greenland, during which they encounter icebergs. Their journey continues to Newfoundland, and two passages describe locales that bear resemblance to the Bahamas and Jamaica.

When the pilgrims reach their goal, they explore inland. An angel tells them that they are close to Paradise and that this country will one day offer a safe haven for those fleeing persecution (a prophecy some see as later fulfilled in the landing of the *Mayflower* and other ships carrying refugees to America).

Some enthusiasts have claimed that, although the story is a fantasy, it is nevertheless based on fact, and that at some early stage in history a contingent of Irish monks did discover America centuries before Christopher Columbus. In 1976 a team of four built a replica of St. Brendan's vessel and set out to see if it was possible to make the voyage. Sailing from County Kerry, Ireland, in May, the crew reached Iceland, and, after wintering there, went on to complete the journey successfully, arriving in Newfoundland in June of the next year.

GREGORY THE GREAT (540–604)

FEAST DAY:	*September 3*
SYMBOLS IN ART:	*Crosier, dove, tiara; pope writing or working on sheet music*
PATRONAGE:	*Choirboys, educators, masons, musicians, singers, school children*
PAINTINGS:	*Isenbrant, Adriaen,* Mass of St. Gregory; *Altar of St. Gregory the Great, Ricci, Sebastiano*
PROFILE:	*Monk, pope, and Doctor of the Western Church*

LEFT *Enthroned in medieval majesty, St. Gregory receives counsel from the dove of divine wisdom while monks of the papal entourage minister below.*

Gregory I stands out as the first great medieval man. Called from his monastery to be Bishop of Rome at the age of 50, he spent the next 14 years strengthening the authority of the papacy. By the time of his death, the Roman Catholic Church had secured its position over and against the imperial Byzantine power at Constantinople, and established itself in the minds of Western Europeans as the source of all authority, spiritual and civil. Gregory openly held himself and his clergy responsible for ordering society and setting its moral standards.

ABOVE Patrons of the arts after the Renaissance looked back on St. Gregory as a force for civilization in barbarian times. His assertion that "painting can do for the illiterate what writing does for those who read" helped the Church to withstand those who opposed religious expression through art.

ARCHITECT OF THE MEDIEVAL PAPACY

By popularizing religious themes, Gregory more than any other theologian created the distinctive character of the medieval church: The cult of the saints, with their bones (relics) and propensity for miraculous cures; the menace of demons; the escape valve of Purgatory, with its souls of the recent dead working off sin like slaves in a spiritual labor camp; and ultimately the virtue of leading an ascetic life. Gregory knew well how to govern susceptible hearts and minds!

KINDLY MONK OR RUTHLESS EVANGELIZER?

Gregory was a keen evangelizer. Of the many problems facing missionaries, one of the most vexing was knowing how to handle the ancient customs of new converts. Gregory's advice to St. Augustine, whom he sent to evangelize the English, was to go gently, accommodating as much as possible. Converts could continue to use their former temples as long as they were sprinkled with holy water. If the people wished to slay cattle as a sacrifice, they could still do so, only now dedicated to God. His thinking that "if we allow them these outward joys, they are more likely to find their way to the true inner joy," set an evangelical style for future missionary work.

However, his tone changed when it came to heathen resistance. Sometimes he openly suggested waging war. In pre-Islamic North Africa, for example, his instruction to convert through aggression was seen as the earliest conception of a crusade, or "holy war."

GREGORIAN CHANT

Gregory is thought to have fostered the development of liturgical music. The monophonic chant, named after him, is sung to accompany the text used in Mass. It was first used widely by Charlemagne, king of the Franks, who imposed it on his kingdom in the eighth century. It became a liturgical norm in Benedictine monasteries.

See also AUGUSTINE *page 140,* BENEDICT *page 50*

AUGUSTINE OF CANTERBURY (DIED C. 604)

FEAST DAY: *May 27*

SYMBOLS IN ART: *Well, baptizing a king*

PATRONAGE: *England*

PAINTINGS: *Coello, Claudio*, The Triumph of St. Augustine; *Guercino*, St. Augustine; *Pacher, Michael*, St. Augustine and St. Gregory; *Piero, Francesca della*, Polyptych of St. Augustine

PROFILE: *First archbishop of Canterbury*

ABOVE *St. Augustine had to convince the Anglo-Saxon King Ethelbert of the truth of Christianity before he could hope to win over the rest of the kingdom.*

THE IDEA OF SENDING A MISSION to convert the English is supposed to have originated when the pope of the time, Gregory the Great, noticed a band of beautiful Anglo-Saxon slave children in the forum at Rome. His words, "They are Angles; let them become angels," trumpeted the call to evangelize their pagan homeland, and duly a mission was dispatched to England under the leadership of Augustine, the prior of Gregory's monastery in Rome.

MISSION TO THE ANGLES

The endeavor was well planned and Augustine departed in 596 with a team of 40 monks—albeit with some trepidation, for the land was then filled with warring Angles, Saxons, and Jutes from barbarian Europe. What existed of Christianity had been pushed to the margins in the Celtic north and west. Indeed, on reaching Gaul (France), the timid Augustine had serious doubts about the idea and pleaded with Gregory to allow him to return to Rome. But the pope was determined the mission should succeed and the request was dismissed out of hand.

However, he should not have feared: The homework had been done. On landing in England the following year, the missionaries were received courteously by the Anglo-Saxon Ethelbert, king of Kent, who had married a Christian princess from Gaul. With Frankish priests among his party as interpreters, Augustine was well set to begin his task. The king himself was a little anxious in case this visiting contingent should be sorcerers and place a spell on his kingdom. With reassurance from his wife, he allowed the missionaries to settle in his capital at Canterbury.

Into the city they marched bearing a cross and banner of Christ before them and singing God's praise. Their virtuous life and preaching made such a deep impression that the king was soon converted. As was the norm in those days, the subjects of the realm wisely followed their master's creed. As Ethelbert was also nominal overlord of the neighboring Anglo-Saxon kingdoms of Essex and East Anglia, by the end of the year three kingdoms had become Christian.

A CHILL WIND FROM THE NORTH

The pope appointed Augustine as the first archbishop of the Church in England, and Ethelbert gave him a palace in Canterbury. Progress from then on was not so swift or even successful. Wars between rival Anglo-Saxon kings hampered the missionary effort, and Augustine's high-handed manner toward leaders of the Celtic Church, whose practices differed from those of Rome, did not help in winning their support.

See also GREGORY THE GREAT *page 72*

COLUMBAN (C. 543–615)

FEAST DAY:	*November 23*
SYMBOLS IN ART:	*Bear*
PATRONAGE:	*None*
PAINTINGS:	*None*
PROFILE:	*Irish missionary to Europe*

PERHAPS THE MOST PIONEERING of all Irish missionaries was St. Columban, who founded religious houses as far south as Italy, including the great medieval monastery of Bobbio, just a few hundred miles from Rome. After he had spent most of his life in Bangor in Northern Ireland, his zeal for a life of voluntary exile, a common aspiration among Irish monks, led him and 11 companions to set out for France in about 590. They knew not what was ahead of them, and they carried a singularly strict brand of the faith. Compared with St. Benedict's gentle version of the monastic life, which would later spread through Europe from Italy, the Rule of St. Columban was like a hardship posting.

GLUTTONS FOR PUNISHMENT

Early Irish monks thrived on harshness: A cold climate, minimal food and sleep, maximum penance; and corporal punishment. A man who misbehaved could be beaten; penance on just bread and water for 40 or 100 days was common; and prayers were said for long periods of time standing with outstretched arms to form the shape of a cross.

MIXED RECEPTION

Columban and his party established monasteries at Luxeuil and Fontaine in the Vosges and seemed to attract a good number of followers. One in his party was St. Gall, who evangelized part of Switzerland, but it was not long before the severity of their practices, as well as other Celtic customs, caused friction with the Frankish Church. Things came to a head when Columban criticized the grandson of Queen Brunhild of Burgundy for his debauchery—he and his compatriots were promptly ordered to leave the country.

However, by good fortune they managed to escape and they decided to continue their mission into Europe.

Rowing up the River Rhine eventually took them to Lake Constance and from here Columban made his way across the Alps into Lombardy in northern Italy. At the considerable age of 70 he helped to build the monastery at Bobbio, which became famous for its large collection of works and its richly illuminated manuscripts in the Celtic style.

ABOVE *A stained glass window from the monastery of Bobbio in north Italy celebrates the monk who spread the Celtic brand of Christianity across Western Europe.*

See also BENEDICT *page 50,* COLUMBA *page 34*

BONIFACE (C. 680–754)

FEAST DAY:	*June 5*
SYMBOLS IN ART:	*Cauldron, club*
PATRONAGE:	*Germany, brewers, tailors*
PAINTINGS:	*None known*
PROFILE:	*English monk who evangelized Germany;* *archbishop of Mainz; martyr*

ABOVE *In a symbolic gesture showing the power of his God, St. Boniface felled the sacred tree of Thor, pagan god of thunder among tribes of early medieval Germany.*

IRISH MISSIONARIES had introduced Christianity to parts of Europe that were still pagan, but it was the Anglo-Saxon monks from England, with their support from Rome, who consolidated these enterprises. Sometimes they had to start again as new generations reverted to the old gods, especially in Germany. But St. Boniface, an English monk, established the faith there once and for all. He became known as the "Apostle to the Germans."

WHERE CHURCHMEN FEARED TO TREAD

Heathen culture still thrived in eighth-century Germany, which had been largely ignored by Rome. Facing a people bent on sacrifices and the worship of nature gods, Boniface armed himself with an ax and marched into a shrine dedicated to Thor, god of thunder. The cult object was a massive oak, and into it the intrepid monk sank his ax. It is said that the tree fell instantly and that the onlookers were so aghast at the power of his God that they all wished to worship him. With the timber, Boniface built a chapel to St. Peter and thus began his conversion of the pagans.

To say that he did away with all superstitious thinking in one fell blow might stretch one's credulity. However, his approach differed from his Celtic predecessors by being tied closely to the authorities in Rome. Boniface personally obtained sanction for his mission from the pope, and then came away with a chest full of saints' relics (bones), fully charged with the potential to effect miraculous cures and victories in battle.

His success was phenomenal, and many from the populations of Hesse, Thuringia, Württemberg, and Bavaria converted. His Benedictine monastery at Fulda still plays a special part in the Catholic Church of Germany today.

REFORMER OF THE FRANKS

The pope called on Boniface to tackle the decadent clergy who served the Merovingian rulers of the Franks (France). A letter of St. Boniface to the pope gives a measure of just how corrupt the medieval church could be:

> *Religion is trodden underfoot. Benefices are given to greedy laymen, or to unchaste clerks. All their crimes do not prevent their attaining the priesthood; at last, rising in rank as they increase in sin, they become bishops, and those who can boast that they are not adulterers or fornicators are drunkards ...*[*]

Acting as their moral guardian, Boniface was able to impose discipline on the Frankish Church and eliminate its worst abuses. By setting this example, the saint initiated a religious revival in Latin Christendom, which other Anglo-Saxon missionaries, including women for the first time, carried through.

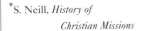

[*] S. Neill, *History of Christian Missions*

See also GREGORY THE GREAT *page 72*

VLADIMIR OF KIEV (C. 955–1015)

FEAST DAY: *July 15*

SYMBOLS IN ART: *Sword, crown*

PATRONAGE: *Converts, murderers, Russia*

PAINTINGS: *None known*

PROFILE: *Prince of Kievan Russia and Apostle of Russia*

RUSSIA OWES ITS CHRISTIAN HERITAGE to St. Vladimir, whose decision to adopt Christianity as the state religion provided posterity with a cultural base that Islam might otherwise have created.

Russia had for centuries been the home of disparate Slavic tribes and cultures; the country had no identity or unity. It was Scandinavian traders plying the long rivers in search of booty who created the first nation of Russia. Their leader was Vladimir, a Viking pagan and marauder. Skirmishes with his own brothers compelled him to come and go from the land before he victoriously established himself as first head of the state of Rus, at Kiev in 980.

FINDING A FAITH

Kievan Russia was a confederation of principalities open to numerous influences—political, religious, cultural—and although it now had political unity it had no identity. According to a chronicle[*] of the time, Vladimir was at a loss as to whom to turn to for advice on which religion would most benefit his subjects. So he sent envoys to various neighbors to investigate their faiths.

They saw Western Christianity in Germany but found the ceremonies too simple. Islam was unappealing, for the Prophet prohibited alcohol, a stricture unlikely to please the Russians. The Jewish faith as practiced by the Khazars also was not suitable. But when the envoys experienced a Byzantine service in Santa Sophia Cathedral in Constantinople they were left in no doubt: "We did not know whether we were in heaven or on earth. It would be impossible to find on earth any splendor greater than this, and it is vain that we attempt to describe it. Never shall we be able to forget so great a beauty."[**]

BYZANTIUM

On seeing this grandeur for himself in 989, Vladimir returned to Russia a Christian and married Anne, daughter of the Byzantine emperor, Basil II. It was a marriage for love but also of diplomacy. A mass baptism of his noble subjects followed, in some cases implemented by force, but the faith spread slowly through the rest of society. Vladimir was committed to reform and was known for his clemency toward murderers and thieves, and providing for the poor, a practice unheard of in Russia.

ABOVE *A monument to Prince Vladimir of Russia, in Kiev, Ukraine.*

The decision of Vladimir to throw in his lot with Constantinople would have lasting significance for the history of Russia. Its own brand of Eastern Orthodoxy developed from the Byzantine Greeks, whose missionaries Vladimir supported in their work among his people. With them they brought the fine elements of Byzantine culture that Slavic Russia adapted to its own: Onion domes and aesthetic masonry; richly ornamented interiors with splendid mosaics; choral music and high-mass liturgy; a literary language and elaborate theology.

[*] *The Chronicle of Nestor*
[**] N. Baynes, *Byzantium*

ABOVE *St. Bernard preaching the Second Crusade (1147–1149) to Louis VII of France at Clairvaux, near Paris. This illustration to a 15th-century manuscript shows the huge numbers prepared to undergo the long journey across Europe to free the Holy Land from occupation by the infidel.*

BERNARD OF CLAIRVAUX (1090–1153)

FEAST DAY:	*August 20*
SYMBOLS IN ART:	*Bees, white dog, chained demon*
PATRONAGE:	*Beekeepers, bees, candle makers*
PAINTINGS:	*Alonso, Cano,* The Vision of St. Bernard; *Lippi, Filippino,* Apparition of the Virgin to St. Bernard; *Perugino, Pietro,* The Vision of St. Bernard; *Ribalta, Francisco,* Christ Embracing St. Bernard
PROFILE:	*Chivalric monk, mystic and "mellifluous" Doctor of the Church; established Cistercian monasticism*

O NE OF THE MOST POWERFUL and fearsome figures of the High Middle wAges was St. Bernard of Clairvaux. Everywhere he chided monks for their idleness. His thunderous condemnation of the leisurely lifestyle of Benedictine monasteries, with their "ridiculous monsters [gargoyles] in the cloister,"* inspired a wholesale rebuilding of the monastic ideal.

THE WHITE MONK

The purity of the religious life was Bernard's aspiration when, aged 22, he entered the lone Cistercian monastery at Cîteaux. He took with him 30 other noblemen from Burgundy, and his leadership qualities were self-evident. He was soon sent to establish a new monastery at Clairvaux, which became one of the chief centers of the new Cistercian order. Bernard believed in hard work, prayer, and self-denial. The strength of his personality and zeal for reform turned him into one of the most influential religious forces of his day. By the time of his death, 40 years later, there were more than 300 Cistercian houses in Europe, all following Bernard's directives. Unlike the urban locations favored by earlier Benedictines, Cistercian monasteries were planted in the wild, and much of the early cultivation of the landscape was their work.

MODEL OF CHIVALRY

Born of a noble family, Bernard exemplified the chivalric ideals of his class. He preached the Second Crusade to the Holy Land (1147). To this end, he took control of the Knights Templar, the organization of Christian soldiers who, robed in their white Cistercian tunics emblazoned with the red cross, gave protection to those undertaking the journey.

Even in this age of courtly love, Bernard had his lady. While praying he is said to have experienced a vision of her, later called the Lactation of the Virgin Mary. As he knelt before the holy image of Mary feeding the infant Jesus, the statue came to life and exuded drops of milk on to his lips.

ON LOVE …

Bernard's faith was inspired by mystical devotion, which he expressed through a number of spiritual hymns still sung today. He believed that Christians came to know God through love, and that prayer and discipline could transform physical love, which was natural, into a redeeming spiritual love.

THE CRUSADES

The Crusades were military missions to recover the Holy Land from Muslim control. The loss of this land, in Christian hands since the fourth century, dealt a shattering blow to Western Christendom. To the medieval mind, Jerusalem was the earthly face of the Jerusalem in Heaven, where the blessed lived, and at all costs it must be recovered. In his preaching of the Second Crusade (1147–1149), St. Bernard of Clairvaux summoned the good and the bad alike, even criminals, to "take the Cross." The reward for a martyr's death was a seat in Heaven, while survivors were promised a new life of prosperity in the East.

* G. Coulton,
A Medieval Garner

See also BENEDICT *page 50*

DOMINIC (1170–1221)

FEAST DAY:	*August 8*
SYMBOLS IN ART:	*Star, black and white dog with torch in its mouth, devil with devotional candle*
PATRONAGE:	*Order of preachers, astronomers*
PAINTINGS:	*Bermejo, Bartolomé, St. Dominic Enthroned in Glory; Coello, Claudio, St. Dominic; Pereda, Antonio de, St. Dominic; Tiziano, Vecellio, St. Dominic*
PROFILE:	*Founder of the Black Friars (Order of Friars Preachers)*

ABOVE *St. Dominic revived an apostolic spirit in banding together friars who, unlike their slothful contemporaries, went out into the world and preached.*

BORN OF A SPANISH NOBLE FAMILY in Castile, Dominic Guzman had done little with his life until, as an Augustinian monk, he was chosen by his bishop to accompany him to southern France to tackle the Albigensian heresy. In executing this task, Dominic discovered his gift for preaching. Using persuasion addressed to the individual's heart and mind, Dominic developed a new kind of missionary approach. It was direct and personal, and an altogether more intellectual style of preaching than that displayed by the other main missionary of the time, St. Francis of Assisi, who tended to emphasize his love of everybody and all creation.

Dominic was an able organizer (again, unlike Francis) and operated from his headquarters in Toulouse. From here he trained itinerant preachers to go out and convert the Albigenses, especially in the Languedoc region, where they were most concentrated. Even when the religious conflict escalated into five years of civil war after the murder of the papal legate, Dominic kept control of his mission despite the massacres and barbarity perpetrated around him.

BEARERS OF ENLIGHTENMENT

When the Dominican Order was founded officially in 1216, friaries started to pop up everywhere. Soon their members filled distinguished teaching posts in Paris and as far away as Oxford. In art his common symbol is a dog holding a torch between its teeth to represent the bearer of the light of knowledge being preached to the ignorant. The dog is a play on words in Latin: Dominicans were nicknamed *domini* canes—dogs of God.

THE DARK LEGACY

Although Dominic himself was deeply compassionate toward his fellow bearers of the faith, whether orthodox or heretical, soon after his death there developed a more sinister side to the intellectual energies of the Dominicans. In continuation of the crusading spirit against heresy, Pope Innocent III established the Inquisition to root out evil heretics wherever they might lurk. The wandering friars who had been well trained by Dominic were the natural choice to serve as inquisitors. The most notorious Grand Inquisitor of all, Torquemada, was a Dominican, and many others filled the roles in Spain where the infidel—Moor or Jew—was common.

EDMUND CAMPION (1540–1581)

FEAST DAY:	*October 25*
SYMBOLS IN ART:	*None*
PATRONAGE:	*None*
PAINTINGS:	*None known*
PROFILE:	*English Jesuit missionary and martyr*

THE PAPAL MISSION of 1580 to bolster the Roman Catholic faith in
Elizabethan England was a virtual death sentence for the Jesuit priest
Edmund Campion. In the minds of English Protestants, Jesuits were the
likely agents of subversive Catholic plots sponsored by the Spanish enemy.
Through great courage and some judicious stealth, Campion was lucky
to last as long as a year before being arrested and charged with treason.

DOUBT AND SUSPICION

Yet he started out his life in the Church of England, an Oxford scholar and
the son of a London bookseller. On being ordained a deacon in 1569, he
began to feel uncertain about his religious affiliation, and it was after a visit
to Ireland (where he helped to found a university in Dublin, later Trinity
College), that he decided to renounce his Anglican faith. However, the pope's
excommunication of Elizabeth I caused widespread ill feeling toward Roman
Catholics and Campion thereafter was watched with suspicion. He returned
to England briefly in disguise, and was stopped while attempting to leave the
country. Only by giving up all his luggage and money was he allowed to go on
his way to Douai in northern France. Here he was admitted into the Roman
Catholic priesthood before going to Rome, where he became a Jesuit in 1573.

THE FATAL MISSION

The Jesuits had been successful in missions across central Europe, so one
was prepared for England. Campion was chosen. He landed at Dover in 1580
disguised as a jewel merchant. But persecution of Catholics in London forced
him to set about his task outside the capital, in Berkshire, Oxfordshire,
Northamptonshire, and Lancashire.

As well as endeavoring to bring Anglicans over to his faith, his role was to
encourage dispirited Catholics. His eloquence, learning, and boldness gave
them heart. Always maintaining a low public profile and keeping on the move,
he covered a lot of ground in a short space of time, disseminating pamphlets
as he went. His most famous work, *Ten Reasons*, was an open challenge to
Protestants to debate the foundations of their faith. Copies were distributed
at a church in Oxford and caused a great sensation. A government already
greatly agitated at Campion's activities now made concerted efforts to catch the
elusive priest, and an extensive house-to-house search finally led to his arrest.

Imprisonment in the Tower of London, bribes, and ultimately torture
all failed to break the missionary. Eventually he was charged with conspiracy
and was sentenced to the method of execution customary for enemies of the
state of being hung, drawn, and quartered. He was canonized by Pope Paul VI
in 1970 and declared one of the Forty Martyrs of England and Wales.

ABOVE *Living with
the enemy, Campion
knew his time would
not be long.*

FRANCIS XAVIER (1506–1552)

FEAST DAY:	*December 3*
SYMBOLS IN ART:	*Bell, crucifix, vessel, torch, flame, cross and lily, globe*
PATRONAGE:	*Roman Catholic missionaries overseas, navigators, the Orient*
PAINTINGS:	*Pozzo, Andrea, St. Francis Xavier*
PROFILE:	*Pioneering Jesuit missionary to the East*

IT IS SAID THAT THE CROSS followed the sword in the colonization of new lands in the sixteenth century. Missionaries in great numbers journeyed to the Americas in the wake of the Spanish conquistadors, yet virtually no one had gone east. The moment came in 1541 for a Basque nobleman by the name of Francis Xavier to undertake such a voyage of discovery to spread the faith. He became known as the "conquistador of souls."

While studying in Paris, Xavier came under the influence of St. Ignatius Loyola and was one of the seven founding Jesuits to dedicate themselves to God on Montmartre (meaning "hill of martyrs"). A deep devotion, coupled with the certain belief that those who died unbaptized would be damned, turned Xavier into a fanatical evangelizer—yet with the discipline of an organized strategist. As well as missionary, he would be international statesman, representing not only the pope but the king of Portugal, with as much power and authority as he needed for this mission, which would extend as far as the Land of the Rising Sun.

INDIA AND THE SPICE ISLANDS

Using the Portuguese Island of Goa as his headquarters from 1542, Xavier conducted missions to south India, in particular to the Coromandel Coast, where an entire caste of pearl fishermen had recently sought protection from the Portuguese against Muslim raiders. The task fell to Xavier to develop the faith beyond their nominal baptism. Although hampered by their language and illiteracy, he nevertheless inculcated sufficient belief for the faith to survive there to the present day.

Xavier spent seven years setting up Christian communities here and in Ceylon (Sri Lanka), the Molucca islands of the East Indies, and on the Malay peninsula. In each place he would live as the poor did, sleeping on the ground in a hut, existing on just rice and water.

JAPAN

Xavier reached his ultimate destination of Japan at a favorable time for outsiders. Foreign trade was encouraged, as were new ideas. A Japanese companion from Goa introduced Xavier to a local ruler who treated them with great courtesy. In contrast with conditions of his previous missions, he found himself circulating among the upper ranks of society and was impressed by the virtues possessed of heathens—good manners, sociability, love of knowledge, and their prizing, above all else, of honor. So much seemed to be noble that Xavier abandoned the standard evangelizing policy of *tabula rasa*, the view that all non-Christian life systems must be razed to the ground before anything Christian could be built. His new approach of building on existing culture proved fruitful for the two years he spent there. However, later in the century, persecution undid most of the missionary's groundwork.

Xavier's attempt to smuggle himself into China, which forbade entry to foreigners, was cut short when he contracted fever at sea and died soon afterwards on the island of Sancian, near mainland China.

See also IGNATIUS LOYOLA *page 58*

SAINT FRANÇOIS-XAVIER.

Né le 7 avril 1506, au Château de Xavier près Pampelune, mort le 2 décembre 1552, âgé de 46 ans, béatifié deux ans après sa mort, et canonisé en 1662. Patron et Protecteur des Indes orientales.

A ÉPINAL, CHEZ PELLERIN, IMPRIMEUR - LIBRAIRE ET FABRICANT DE CARTES A JOUER.

ABOVE *A Portuguese merchant beckons his slaves to help the dying St. Francis, as his Chinese friend Antony administers the last rites.*

JOSEPH OF CUPERTINO (1603–1663)

FEAST DAY:	*September 18*
SYMBOLS IN ART:	*None*
PATRONAGE:	*Flying, air travelers, aircraft pilots, astronauts*
PAINTINGS:	*None*
PROFILE:	*Franciscan priest and mystic, famous for levitation and miraculous healing*

ABOVE *Joseph of Cupertino is believed to have performed more acts of levitation than anyone else in Christian history.*

FOR 35 YEARS this humble Italian friar was kept out of the public eye. Joseph of Cupertino in southern Italy was not allowed to celebrate Mass or even eat meals with his brethren. Such disturbing phenomena surrounded his daily life that his superiors regarded his presence as detrimental to the welfare of the community. His "crime" was to be the subject of ecstatic trances, miraculous healing power, and levitation, to which such witnesses as the philosopher Leibnitz and a papal ambassador have attested.

HUMBLE ORIGINS
Born in a stable to a poor woman whose husband had died during the pregnancy, Joseph had a difficult early life. He was mocked at school for being slow and having a gaping mouth. Despite little education, Joseph was accepted by a local Franciscan monastery, and it was there, as a stable boy, that his life began to change. He became assiduous, hard-working, and devoted to religious duty.

"THE FLYING FRIAR"
After his ordination to the priesthood at the age of 25, Joseph led a mystical life, sometimes experiencing visions and heavenly music in a state of religious ecstasy. Perhaps most amazing were his alleged feats of levitation, the raising of the body through the air without any apparent physical force. During the 17 years he stayed at the Franciscan monastery of Grotella, there are recorded no fewer than 70 such instances, the most that any saint is said to have achieved.

Several times Joseph would be taking part in collective prayer, kneeling at the altar rail, when, it is claimed, his brethren would become aware that he was rising from the floor. Some accounts describe him flying through the air, earning him the nickname of "the Flying Friar," and the patronage of airplane travel. His acts of levitation would always be accompanied by a state of ecstasy. No amount of pin-pricking and blows, even of burning his skin, would rouse him from his trance.

SUSPICION OF THE REACTIONARIES
These phenomena attracted attention beyond the monastery walls with varying receptions, some fearing a sinister presence. Joseph was first sent to appear before the Inquisition of Naples, but his humility and innocence confounded his examiners. He was eventually sent to appear before Pope Urban VIII and promptly fell into ecstasy. The pope was sure he had witnessed a miracle.

Despite clearing his name, Joseph was kept in seclusion for the rest of his life. It is said that, at Joseph's death, his doctor noted that he was floating six inches above the bed and uttering that at last he could smell the fragrance of Paradise.

See also TERESA OF AVILA *page 120*

KATHERINE DREXEL (1858–1955)

FEAST DAY:	*March 3*
SYMBOLS IN ART:	*None*
PATRONAGE:	*None*
PAINTINGS:	*None*
PROFILE:	*Heiress and missionary to black and Native Americans*

ABOVE *The mission without frontiers.*

AN IMMENSE FAMILY FORTUNE enabled Katherine Drexel to put into action what her conscience demanded. While families in her social class led happy and prosperous lives, their compatriots elsewhere in the United States suffered depredations unthinkable in well-to-do Philadelphia. Katherine's own parents were philanthropic and had shown her the way of charity by opening up their house to the poor for two days a week to distribute food, clothing, and rent assistance. But it was a trip with her father to the poor northwest territories of the United States that opened her eyes to the suffering of Native Americans with their virtual absence of civil rights.

MISSION TO MINORITY AMERICANS

The death of her father soon after this trip, coupled with a prolonged period of nursing her stepmother through cancer, took its emotional toll. Yet the sorrow played its part in making her more determined than ever to ameliorate the lives of those in need, and she vowed to dedicate her inheritance to helping Native Americans.

An audience with Pope Leo XIII settled her mind and she took holy vows with a view to becoming a missionary. She instituted a charitable organization, the Sisters of Blessed Sacrament, dedicated to the relief of poor black and Native Americans. She traveled to the Dakotas, befriended a Sioux chieftain, and began her systematic program of aid. After the government's failed promises of providing education for them, Katherine built a network of rural schools, churches, and missions especially for them, paying the salaries of local black teachers.

HER LEGACY

By 1942, Katherine Drexel had constructed a system of black and Native American Catholic schools in 13 states, and had established 40 mission centers and 50 Native American missions for her successors to continue her work. She also financed Xavier University in New Orleans, the first university for blacks, which sends more black American graduates to medical school than any other in the country. At her death, aged 96, there were more than 500 sisters teaching at 63 schools throughout the United States. She was canonized by Pope John Paul II in 2000.

CROSSING SOCIAL BARRIERS

Katherine Drexel was about 70 years ahead of her time. The recent Civil War (1861–1865), fought over the issue of black slavery in the South, had left bitter feelings, and her conviction of social justice for all was not shared by everyone around her. Some Southern states tried to prevent her schools from employing black teachers. And, when she tried to fill churches with ethnically mixed congregations, the Klu Klux Klan threatened violence.

CHAPTER 5

DISASTER
AND
RESCUE

MICHAEL THE ARCHANGEL

FEAST DAY:	*September 29 (Michaelmas Day)*
SYMBOLS IN ART:	*Dragon, sword, weighing scales*
PATRONAGE:	*Christians, soldiers, policemen, the sick and dying, ambulance drivers, emergency medical personnel, paratroopers, radiologists, holy death, boatmen, security guards, artists, bakers, grocers, coopers, haberdashers, milliners, temptations, Israel, Germany, Sicily*
PAINTINGS:	*Giordano, Luca,* Casting the Rebel Angels Into the Abyss; *Memling, Hans,* The Archangel Michael; *Raphael,* Trampling the Dragon; *Zenale,* St. Michael
PROFILE:	*Angelic defender of the faith; often venerated on mountaintops*

FROM THE BEGINNING of Christian history the Archangel Michael has been honored as a defender of the faith. The theme of an angelic guardianship of God's people has its roots in Jewish history, and continued into the Christian era with his appearance in the Book of Revelation, in which he leads the army of God against the uprising of Lucifer in a "war of heaven." In the Western Church, Michael was adopted as the protector of Christians in general, and soldiers in particular; while the Eastern Church came to regard him as a special guardian of the sick after he caused a medicinal spring to spout at Chairotopa, near Colossae, in present-day Turkey. All the sick who bathed there were cured, and hence he is now patron to many medical professions.

Michael presides over worship during Mass, sending the prayers of the faithful to God, as symbolized by the smoke from incense. He is also intermediary to departed souls, ushering them to the afterlife, and along the way weighing the souls for righteousness—hence his symbolism in art with weighing scales and his adoption by occupations such as grocers and bakers. He guards the gates of Purgatory and receives prayers made for the unfortunate souls therein.

ANGELS AND ARCHANGELS

When holy spirits of Heaven deliver a message they are called angels. According to Gregory the Great (540–604), those who deliver messages of lesser importance are angels; those who proclaim messages of supreme importance are archangels. For example, Gabriel is regarded as an archangel because he announced the incarnation to Mary. Angels merely concerned with individuals' needs are often referred to as guardian angels.

APPARITIONS OF ST. MICHAEL

Numerous apparitions of Michael have been reported over the centuries, usually near mountaintops:

- The Michaelion Church, near Constantinople, was built by Emperor Constantine in gratitude to St. Michael for his defeat of the pagan enemy Maxentius. Many miracles have allegedly occurred at the church.
- A vision of Michael was seen at Monte Gargano in southern Italy toward the end of the fifth century.
- This vision gave rise to the legends of Mont Saint Michel in France, St. Michael's Mount in England, and at the Stranberg in Germany.
- During a plague in Rome, Pope Gregory the Great is said to have seen the archangel sheathing a sword above Hadrian's mausoleum (now called the Castle of St. Angelo).
- In Spain, an apparition to a shepherd boy in the foothills of the Sierra de Guadarrama carried a message to build a shrine and found a brotherhood.

MICHAELMAS DAY

His feast in the Middle Ages was a holy day. In some countries it is one of the quarterly days for settling accounts. Families prepared a stubble goose for this feast day, as it was considered to have reached perfection by about this time. Some parishes (for example, the Isle of Skye) conducted a procession and baked a cake, called St. Michael's bannock.

See also THOMAS AQUINAS *page 24,* GEORGE *page 94,* GREGORY THE GREAT *page 72*

LEFT *In the Apocalypse of St. John, the Archangel Michael fought with the dragon before it was cast into the world as the devil. A Renaissance depiction of the encounter has Michael weighing the fiendish soul at the moment of death.*

MARY MAGDALENE (FIRST CENTURY)

FEAST DAY: *July 22*

SYMBOLS IN ART: *Alabaster box of ointment*

PATRONAGE: *Penitent women, people ridiculed for their piety, perfumers, glove makers, hairdressers, tanners, contemplative life, sexual temptation*

PAINTINGS: *Beckmann, Max,* Christ and the Woman Taken in Adultery; *Giotto,* Christ Appearing to Mary Magdalene; *Caravaggio,* The Repentant Magdalene; *Poussin, Nicolas,* Mary Magdalene Anointing Jesus's Feet

PROFILE: *Friend and follower of Jesus; first to see the risen Christ*

ABOVE *St. Mary Magdalene Repentant, c.1530.*

T HE NOTORIOUS "SINNER" of the New Testament became history's icon of the penitent woman. The very name Magdalene has given rise to its own meaning of *maudlin*—one who is tearfully emotional. In fact, the name derives from the Galilean coastal town of Magdala, where she lived. Traditionally she is identified with the woman taken in adultery, an episode in which Jesus challenges her indignant executioners with the words, "He that is without sin among you, let him first cast a stone at her" (John 8:7). The other significant passage to involve Mary occurs at Simon the Pharisee's house when she first washes Jesus's feet with her tears, then anoints them with oil.

Famous though these passages are, in neither of them is Mary's name stated, so there is a problem of identity. Some consider her to be the Mary of Bethany, sister of Martha and Lazarus. However, Mary was a common name and there is no reason to suppose it was Magdalene. St. Luke does describe Mary Magdalene as being a follower of Jesus and one "out of whom went seven devils" (Luke 8:2). Elsewhere in the Gospels she is named as one of the three women who witness Jesus's dying on the cross (Mark 15), and she is the first person to whom the risen Christ appeared in the Garden of Gethsemane (John 20).

FACT OR TRADITION?

There has been some confusion in history over just what Mary Magdalene did or did not do. Ever since Pope Gregory the Great declared that the woman who was taken in adultery, who anointed Jesus's feet, and who first saw the risen Christ, were all one and the same person, history has dealt Mary a poor hand. By contrast with the Roman Catholic Church, Eastern Orthodoxy has kept the three figures apart—Mary Magdalene was not the prostitute that Catholics believe her to be. Her historical misrepresentation is gradually being recognized and today she is regarded as foremost among Jesus's followers.

POPULAR ICON

Not only was Mary Magdalene influential on generations of people in antiquity, but she appears frequently in popular culture. She has become an icon for feminism, feminist spirituality, and sexual liberation, regardless of the accuracy of her status as a "whore." She is a symbol of feminine wisdom, perfect love, and also of sorrow. The representations of Magdalene are almost as limitless as the imaginations of those to whom her legend has presented itself

ABOVE *The risen Christ appears to Mary Magdalene but does not permit her touch.*

AGATHA (THIRD CENTURY)

FEAST DAY: *February 5*

SYMBOLS IN ART: *Breasts on a dish, candle, hand in flame, pincers, tongs*

PATRONAGE: *Protection against fire and eruption of Mount Etna; earthquakes, breast diseases; bell makers, rape victims*

PAINTINGS: *Bonone, Carlo,* St. Stephen and St. Agatha

PROFILE: *Sicilian virgin who spurned advances from her suitor*

FESTIVALS OF SAINTS

❖

Most towns in Roman Catholic countries can turn to their own patron saints for protection. If they are situated in dangerous locations, such as in the shadow of an active volcano, or on seismic fault lines, the festivities may be even more joyous as the inhabitants celebrate the passing of another year in safety. In the case of Catania, Agatha's silver sarcophagus is borne in procession through the streets of the town. Elsewhere statues may be carried, dressed in fine robes and decorated with flowers. A religious service is held, usually followed in the evening by a gala of singing, dancing, and fireworks.

THERE WERE A NUMBER of young female saints of the third and fourth centuries, such as Lucy of Syracuse and Agnes of Rome. Also famous was Agatha, whose feast day still commemorates the saving of her home town of Catania from destruction.

AVERTING STREAMS OF LAVA

According to tradition, about a year after Agatha's death, Mount Etna erupted and threatened to engulf the town with molten lava. Terrified inhabitants ran for their lives but some put their trust in the local saint. They took Agatha's veil from her tomb and stood defiantly in the path of the oncoming lava, praying for her aid. It is said that miraculously the lava altered its course at the last minute and passed by Catania, sparing the inhabitants certain death.

ABOVE *In a painting by Carlo Bonone (1569–1632), an angel descends with the palm leaves of martyrdom to console St. Agatha, who holds up a cup containing her severed breasts.*

HIGH PRICE OF VIRTUE

This girl saint became associated with natural disasters after an earlier earthquake coincided with her unjust death—the one event being seen as a divine punishment for the other. She had suffered horribly in prison through no fault of her own. Her brief life had been a model of Christian devotion, but, when she turned down an offer of marriage, her humiliated suitor, a Roman consul, had her arrested for being a Christian (an offense at the time).

Among her many gruesome tortures was the mutilation of her breasts, which has given rise to curious representations in art. Sometimes she is depicted carrying them on a dish; their resemblance to bells gave rise to her patronage of bell makers. Others considered them to look like small loaves of bread, which explains the custom observed in many churches of blessing bread in church on her feast day.

JANUARIUS (DIED C.305)

FEAST DAY:	*September 19*
SYMBOLS IN ART:	*None*
PATRONAGE:	*Volcanic eruptions, blood banks, Naples*
PAINTINGS:	*None known*
PROFILE:	*Bishop of Benevento and martyr*

PRESERVED IN THE CATHEDRAL at Naples is a glass vial containing a substance traditionally held to be the dried blood of the martyr St. Januarius. Every year on the saint's feast day thousands of devotees gather in the cathedral and its square to await the cardinal's verdict on whether the blood has liquefied. According to tradition, the liquefaction is a sign of assurance that the year will be free from disasters—and the quicker the process is completed the better the following year will be!

MIRACULOUS BLOOD OF A MARTYR

This curious phenomenon, with no known explanation, is regarded as a miracle that has occurred for the last 500 years. There is no mention of the relic before 1389, more than a thousand years after Januarius was martyred during the persecution of Emperor Diocletian. Little more is known about the saint, except that he was Bishop of Benevento, in southern Italy, and his relics were transported to Naples in the fifth century.

The saint's patronage of Naples is dated by the anniversary of the eruption of Mount Vesuvius in 1631, which is said to have ceased after the city's faithful prayed to their patron. One of the few years in which the liquefaction did not occur was 1939, the year when World War II began. Cardinals of Naples have since used the occasion to pray for wisdom among the world's leaders in averting conflicts.

A CLAMMY HOAX?

The phenomenon has attracted its share of critics who claim that there is wax mixed in the blood, which melts from the heat. However, the substance in the vial liquefies irrespective of the season, on feast days in May, September, and December. It also appears to behave inconsistently. The speed of the liquefaction bears no relation to temperature and the weight and volume of the substance can vary. The liquefaction of Januarius's blood has been known not to occur during the December feast, much to the irritation of his devotees. Similar transformations of martyrs' blood have been recorded in other places, nearly all in southern Italy, and some are clearly spurious.

LEFT *A scene from the life of St. Januarius, painted c.1610, warns of the destructive power of Mount Vesuvius.*

GEORGE (FOURTH CENTURY)

FEAST DAY:	*April 23*
SYMBOLS IN ART:	*White flag with red cross, dragon, lance*
PATRONAGE:	*Soldiers, farmers, armorers; protector against plague, leprosy and syphilis; England, Germany, Portugal*
PAINTINGS:	*Carpaccio, Vittore,* St. George and the Dragon; *Correggio* Madonna with St. George; *Dürer, Albrecht,* St. George; *Raffaello, Sanzio,* St. George Fighting the Dragon; *Tintoretto,* St. George and the Dragon; *Uccello, Paulo,* St. George and the Dragon
PROFILE:	*Soldier and martyr; one of the Fourteen Holy Helpers; cult reduced to local status by Roman Catholic Church in 1969*

HONOR AND GALLANTRY

❖

King Edward III of England (from 1327–1377) made George the patron saint of his country and founded the Order of the Garter for 40 "men of knightly renown." The honor still lies as the personal gift of the sovereign, who chooses a replacement on the death of a member. On the feast day members attend a service at St. George's Chapel in Windsor. In 1940 George VI of England instituted a medal, the George Cross, to be awarded to civilians who have put their lives at risk for others. Among the 45 recipients have been bomb-disposal experts and mine clearers.

THIS PALESTINIAN CHRISTIAN SOLDIER, martyred in Lydda during the persecution of Emperor Diocletian (beginning in 305), is now best known for his legend of slaying a dragon. His cult became highly popular in the Middle Ages, as much in the East as in the West, especially during the Crusades. He came to personify the ideals of Christian chivalry, and the expression "my knight in shining armor" is derived largely from him.

VANQUISHER OF ENEMIES

As a soldier-saint he was believed to help in battle. From early times, George was the patron of Byzantine armies. A vision of him during the First Crusade was reported by returning soldiers, and led Richard the Lionheart to place himself and his army under the saint's protection for the Third Crusade. Subsequent troops rallied to the cry of "St. George for England," including the Battle of Agincourt when Henry V invoked his aid. The last "sighting" of the saint in a military capacity was during World War I when, mounted on a white charger, he was reported to have led a line of angelic bowmen in a rout of German troops in the Battle of Mons.

THE DRAGON SLAYER

The legend derives from Lydda near Jaffa. A dragon terrorized people by breathing poisonous fumes wherever it roamed. It was appeased by the offer of two sheep each day, but when they grew scarce a human sacrifice was made instead. When the lot fell to the king's daughter, she nobly accepted her fate dressed as a bride. George intervened and pierced the dragon with his lance. Thereafter, the beast was a tame captive, led by the princess's girdle. George assured the people that all would be well if they served Christ. They agreed and were baptized, and in return he slew the dragon.

RIGHT *St. George killing the dragon, designed as a letterhead by Heywood Sumner, 1892.*

See also BLAISE *page 32,* MARTIN OF TOURS *page 137*

ABOVE *By the 15th century, when this Russian
icon was made, St. George had become a model
of Christian chivalry and was widely venerated.*

LEO THE GREAT (DIED 461)

FEAST DAY:	*November 10*
PATRONAGE:	*None*
PAINTINGS:	*Raffaello, Sanzio, The Meeting Between Leo the Great and Attila (Fresco)*
PROFILE:	*Italian pope and Doctor of the Church*

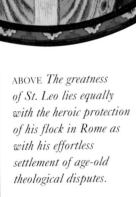

IN HIS 21 YEARS AS POPE, Leo I is remembered for widely differing achievements. To problems as varied as a theological debate on the nature of Christ and the menace of Attila the Hun before the gates of Rome, he applied the same single-minded determination to find a workable solution. Indeed, his utterances on any matter he chose to address seemed so simple and effective that they were thought to be the direct inspiration of St. Peter, his apostolic predecessor.

A letter he had written to a fellow clergyman was used at the Council of Chalcedon (451) as the basis for settling the age-old dispute on the twin natures of God and man possessed of Christ. Other correspondence also served as authority for later confirming the primacy of the papacy in the Roman Catholic Church. His phrases describing the pope's position (with "plenitude of power"), and that of the role of the bishop ("sharing in his responsibility"*), slid so easily into current usage that they became established before anyone asked what exactly they meant.

DEFENDER OF ROME

Perhaps of more importance to the citizens of Rome was Leo's gift for diplomacy. In 452 the Huns of Central Asia entered Italy under the leadership of the fearsome Attila. He burned and slaughtered all before him, and the capital was next in line. With a nervous company of priests Leo set out to meet the invader face to face. His charm—and a bribe—were sufficient to persuade Attila to spare the city.

Leo was less successful three years later, when the next enemy at the gate was not as receptive to his bribery. He could not stop the Vandals occupying and pillaging Rome, but he did prevent a massacre and the wholesale burning of monuments. Many captives were taken back to Carthage in North Africa to be enslaved and Leo sent them priests and alms to reduce their suffering.

Although his pontificate was occasioned by the sacking of the imperial city, the Roman clergy were probably grateful that such an indomitable character of great magnanimity should have held the See at such a brutal time.

ABOVE *The greatness of St. Leo lies equally with the heroic protection of his flock in Rome as with his effortless settlement of age-old theological disputes.*

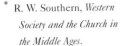

* R. W. Southern, *Western Society and the Church in the Middle Ages.*

GENEVIÈVE (C.422–C.500)

FEAST DAY:	*January 3*
SYMBOLS IN ART:	*Bread, candle, shepherd's crook*
PATRONAGE:	*Protector against disasters, fever, and plague; Paris*
PAINTINGS:	*None known*
PROFILE:	*Devout visionary who protected Paris from siege and epidemic*

WHILE STILL A GIRL of seven, Geneviève was marked for her sanctity. The local bishop, St. Germanus, blessed the girl and told her parents about her special vocation, of how she would become a prophetess and possess special powers invested in her by the Holy Spirit.

When she was 15, she "took the veil" of holiness in Paris and began a life dedicated to Christ. She devoted herself to works of charity and fasted all week except for two meals, on Thursdays and Sundays, which consisted of barley bread and beans. She followed this routine for 30 years. Despite her sacrificial life, neighbors accused her of being an impostor and a hypocrite, no doubt jealous of her visions and prophecies, which they claimed were fraudulent. They were about to cast her into a river when the bishop who had spotted her in early life came to her rescue. This holy woman, he exclaimed, was possessed of the power to save the city from impending disaster.

MENACE OF THE HUN

A fearsome army from the East led by Attila the Hun was overrunning Europe in the fifth century, and now appeared to have set its sights on Paris. Geneviève urged its inhabitants to trust in God and do works of penance. Instead of fleeing the city, they heeded her words, and a strange calm descended while hooves pounded in the distance. With eyes shut tight in supplication, the citizens of Paris waited and waited, only to discover that Attila had turned south to Orléans. Their city had been spared.

Another occasion of peril was the Franks' blockade of the city. Geneviève is credited with organizing a convoy of barges to navigate the Seine to towns upstream in order to procure provisions for its starving population. When she returned with her boats laden with corn, once again she was the people's darling. Despite the fall of the city to the Frankish Childeric, her pleas of mercy on behalf of the prisoners of war were well received and many lives were spared.

Ever since the death of St. Geneviève, Parisians have seen the hand of their protectress at work. In 1129 an epidemic of ergot poisoning, the "burning sickness," was suddenly brought under control after her relics were borne in a procession through the streets of the capital. This event is still commemorated each year in its churches.

ABOVE *The holiness of St. Geneviève of Nanterre, near Paris, brought peace to all who lay within her circle of influence.*

EDWARD THE CONFESSOR (C.1003–1066)

FEAST DAY: *October 13*
SYMBOLS IN ART: *Finger ring*
PATRONAGE: *Difficult marriages, kings, England (formerly)*
PAINTINGS: *None known*
PROFILE: *Devout king of England*

ABOVE *Edward the Confessor on his Anglo-Saxon throne, in the style of the Bayeux Tapestry.*

CULT OF A NATIONAL ICON

❖

A tradition of Edward's appearance—developed from the Bayeux Tapestry, which recorded the Norman Conquest—helped to turn the honorable saint into a national icon. Depicted as a tall man with a long, ruddy face and ash-blond hair, he vied only with St. George for patronage of England. At the siege of Calais in 1351, soldiers prepared for the final assault by invoking both saints to deliver the enemy into their hands.
The Confessor is reputed also to have seen visions and miraculously cured an ailment called king's scrofula (tuberculosis of the lymph nodes) by his touch.

EDWARD'S TITLE refers to his Christian piety, which won the hearts of his subjects at a time when holding on to the English crown was fraught with danger. At the age of ten he had to flee to Normandy with his French mother after the Danes had killed his father, Ethelred the Unready, and seized the throne. He did not set foot in England again until he was over 40, when a political wind of change summoned him to be king. Two years after his coronation Edward married, somewhat in deference to his subjects' wishes, the daughter of Godwin, Earl of Wessex, a wedlock that was reputed to be celibate; certainly it produced no heir.

Precisely who should succeed Edward was a thorny question that dogged much of his reign. His rule brought relative peace and justice to his people for 20 years, but at a price, for his death inadvertently brought about the Norman invasion of 1066. He had apparently promised the throne to William of Normandy (the Conqueror) when he visited England in 1051. This almost caused a civil war with Edward's powerful father-in-law, and on his deathbed the exhausted king relented and named Godwin's son, Harold, as the new monarch.

FOUNDER OF WESTMINSTER ABBEY

The aspiration of every devout Christian in the Middle Ages was to make the pilgrimage to Jerusalem to visit the sacred sites of the Passion. Edward vowed to make such a journey but when events of his kingship overtook him he sought the pope's advice. Edward was told to put as much money as he would have spent on the journey to the cause of the needy and to endow a monastery. He chose a small abbey by the River Thames, rebuilt it in a grand Romanesque style, and named it West Minster to distinguish it from the cathedral in east London, St. Paul's. The royal abbey was destined to become the place of coronation and burial for future kings and queens of England.

See also GEORGE *page 94*

BERNARD OF AOSTA (DIED 1081)

FEAST DAYS:	*May 28*
SYMBOLS IN ART:	*White dog*
PATRONAGE:	*Mountaineers, mountain travelers*
PAINTINGS:	*Cano, Alonso,* The Vision of St. Bernard; *Lippi, Filippino,* Apparition of the Virgin to St. Bernard; *Ribalta, Francisco,* Christ Embracing St. Bernard
PROFILE:	*Priest and eponymous founder of rescue dogs*

THE MAN WHO DID THE MOST to help and protect travelers crossing the Alps in the Middle Ages was St. Bernard, born in Menthon. When he became archdeacon of Aosta in Italy, his diocese extended over vast mountainous terrain, with many of its scattered inhabitants living in remote places. He visited them all on a regular basis in all weather for over 40 years.

His legacy includes two rest houses built at the summits of the high Alpine passes named after him, the Little and Great St. Bernard. The weary and the lost would be accommodated and fed. Many lives would have been lost but for the service offered by the Austin canons who manned these hospices, and still do today. The two main threats to trans-Alpine travelers, many of whom were pilgrims to Rome, were snowdrifts and robbers living in the mountains. There was nothing he could do about the former, but it is said he made the passes safe from the latter.

After Bernard's death, a breed of dog trained to search for victims and used for rescue operations was named after him. Bernard was made patron of mountain climbers in 1923 by Pope Pius XI, himself a mountaineer.

ST. BERNARD RESCUE DOGS

The Austin friars who continued the hospice work of St. Bernard first used dogs in mountain-rescue operations in the seventeenth century. The powerful breed is perfectly adapted to freezing Alpine conditions. Possibly originating from the Tibetan Mastiff brought to Europe by the Romans, the brown and white dog is sure-footed on snow and ice, and has the stamina needed for lengthy expeditions.

Its heightened sense of smell enables it to sniff out people buried in the snow; it also appears to be endowed with a sixth sense about impending storms and avalanches. Some 2,500 lifesaving operations have been achieved. The dog's qualities of gentleness, patience, and loyalty are surely the virtues any saint would be pleased to possess.

BELOW *A statue of St. Bernard in the abbey at Mont du Cats, France.*

MALACHY OF ARMAGH (1094-1148)

FEAST DAY: *November 3*
SYMBOLS IN ART: *Offering an apple to a king*
PATRONAGE: *None*
PAINTINGS: *None*
PROFILE: *Archbishop, healer, and prophet by tradition*

ABOVE *The saint who is said to have envisioned every pope from his day to the end of the world.*

---

* Terry H. Jones,
"St. Malachy O'Muro"
(www.catholic-
forum.com/saints).

A FRIEND OF ST. BERNARD of Clairvaux, Malachy introduced the Cistercian model of monastic life to Ireland in 1142. Much of his energy was devoted to bringing the traditional Celtic Church into line with the Church of Rome. His character and spiritual power were admired by Bernard, who wrote his biography. The Irish bishop was said to have the power to cure illnesses simply by laying his hands on the heads of the afflicted.

Of lasting fame, though of doubtful authenticity, are his so-called "Prophecies." Some say they were written by a forger in the sixteenth century. Other records assert that in 1139 he received a vision showing him all the popes from his day until the end of the world, and that he wrote a poetic description of each one. The manuscript was supposed to have been presented to Pope Innocent II and then put away until the sixteenth century. The "Prophecies" have caused a good deal of controversy ever since. According to these writings, there are only two popes remaining after John Paul II.

PROPHETIC VISIONS OF THE LAST POPES

● The 108th pope to follow Innocent II is described in Latin as the "Flower of Flowers." The corresponding pope was Paul VI (1963–1978), whose coat-of-arms consisted of three fleurs-de-lis (iris flowers).

● The 109th pope is described as "Of the Half Moon." The corresponding pope was John Paul I (1978), who was born in the diocese of Belluno (meaning "beautiful Moon") and was christened Albino Luciani (meaning "white light"). He became pope on August 26 1978, when the Moon appeared exactly half full, and he died the following month shortly after an eclipse of the Moon.

● The 110th pope is "Of the Solar Eclipse" or "From the Toil of the Sun," and refers to John Paul II (1978–present) who was born on May 8, 1920 during an eclipse of the Sun. Like the Sun, he came from the East (Poland) and has gradually worked his way around the globe, visiting more countries than any other pope in history.

● The 111th pope is "The Glory of the Olive." The Order of St. Benedict, whose members are known as the Olivetans, has claimed that this pope will be drawn from their ranks. St. Benedict himself prophesied that before the end of time his order will be triumphant in leading the Catholic Church in its fight against evil.

● The 112th prophecy says, "In the final persecution of the Holy Roman Church there will reign Petrus Romanus [Peter the Roman], who will feed his flock amid many tribulations; after which the city of seven hills will be destroyed, and the dreadful Judge will judge the people. The End." *

FERDINAND III OF CASTILE (C. 1199–1252)

FEAST DAY: *May 30*
SYMBOLS IN ART: *Greyhound*
PATRONAGE: *Prisoners, rulers, magistrates, paupers, Seville, Spain*
PAINTINGS: *None*
PROFILE: *Spanish king of Castile who liberated Andalusía from the Moors*

WHEN FERDINAND BECAME KING of Castile in 1217, the southern half of Spain remained under Islamic control, as it had been since the Moors from North Africa overran the country 500 years earlier. When Ferdinand also inherited the crown of Leon in 1230, he set his mind to continuing what his father had begun, of leading the crusade to liberate the rest of Spain. He spent 27 years warring with the Moors and by the time of his death only the kingdom of Granada was still in Muslim hands.

BELOW The Spanish Ferdinand III, a rare example of a warrior king being accorded the status of a saint.

RECONQUEST OF ANDALUSÍA

The great landmarks of Ferdinand's military achievements were the capture of the cities of Córdoba (1236) and Seville (1248). In both places he turned the great mosques into cathedrals. In every successive town that he captured he re-established Catholic worship, had churches and monasteries built, and financed hospitals.

His military stance, though determined, was not cruel and he treated prisoners and his new subjects with respect. Keeping a watchful eye on the conduct of his soldiers was one priority as he went about the battle camp more like a monk in a cloister than a triumphant leader.

He wore a hair shirt in self-mortification, fasted, and often spent nights in prayer, especially before battle. It is said that his army was led into the Battle of Xeres by the Apostle St. James, who was regarded as the great deliverer of Spain in its long struggle against the infidel. The outcome was so victorious that only 12 Spaniards lost their lives.

KING OF THREE RELIGIONS

Unlike his much later heirs to the Spanish throne, Ferdinand imposed no imperative of conversion on his new Muslim and Jewish subjects, though he encouraged the friars in their missionary work. The Muslim Emir of Granada acknowledged Ferdinand as his sovereign and cooperated with his administration, which was widely recognized for its impartial justice and clemency to those who opposed the crown. He strove to improve the lives of his people and bind them into a cohesive nation.

Ferdinand was buried in Seville dressed not in royal robes but in the habit of a Franciscan friar. The cult of this devout warrior king became popular soon after his death.

See also JAMES "THE GREATER" *page 64*

CATHERINE OF SIENA (1347–1380)

FEAST DAY:	*April 29*
SYMBOLS IN ART:	*Crown of thorns, ring, lily, stigmata*
PATRONAGE:	*Protector against fire and illness; firefighters, nurses, sexual temptation, Italy, Siena, Rome, Europe*
PAINTINGS:	*de Siena, Barna,* Mystical Marriage of Saint Catherine; *Fra Bartolomeo,* Marriage of Catherine of Siena; *Pinturicchio,* The Canonization of Catherine of Siena
PROFILE:	*Italian mystic and Doctor of the Church*

ABOVE *St. Catherine, patron saint of Italy.*

RECEIVING THE STIGMATA

❖

In 1375 Catherine had a spiritual experience in Pisa. After taking communion she was rapt in meditation before the crucifix when suddenly five blood-red rays seemed to issue from it and pierce her hands, feet, and heart, causing such pain that she fainted. The wounds, which were invisible, remained as stigmata for the last five years of her life, and became clearly visible after her death.

THE CO-PATRON of Italy (with St. Francis of Assisi) and of Europe (with St. Benedict) is one of the best loved of Roman Catholic saints. St. Catherine's mystical devotion and resolute conviction in fighting for religious truth prompted Pope Paul II to describe her as an admirable "synthesis between contemplation and action."

MYSTICAL UNION WITH CHRIST

This youngest of 25 children born to a cloth-dyer in Siena is said to have had her first vision of Jesus at the age of six. Deep devotion and solitude through her childhood were followed by another vision, 13 years later, while she was praying in her room on Shrove Tuesday. According to Catherine's testimony, the Virgin Mary took her hand and held it up to Christ who placed a ring upon one finger and declared the girl to be his bride. She was told to take courage in forthcoming adversity. Thereafter, the ring remained visible to her but invisible to others.

RECOVERY OF THE PAPACY

Catherine's reputation for holiness won her many followers, both among the Dominicans, whom she had joined, and the laity; she called them all her "family." Her spirituality rubbed off on others, sometimes changing people's lives, and often healing feuds. Her ability as a mediator brought her into the arena of church politics. At this time the papal residence lay in Avignon, and pressure was mounting on Pope Gregory XI to return to Rome. It was Catherine who finally persuaded him to act, thus ending 74 years of absence.

Her greatest public challenge was to come in the form of the Great Schism. The removal of the papacy from Avignon did not prevent French bishops from electing their own successor to Gregory on his death two years later, as a rival to the new pope chosen in Rome. Once again, Catherine made use of her mediating skills, dictating numerous letters (for she was illiterate) to both camps in a bid for recognition of the true pontiff. She was eventually called to Rome to help resolve the matter but in a short time suffered a seizure, in which she had a vision of a ship of the Church crushing her to the Earth. Soon thereafter she had a stroke and died. The rift in the Catholic Church rumbled on for 40 years. Catherine was declared a Doctor of the Church in 1970.

See also FRANCIS OF ASSISI *page 38*

ABOVE *Despite opposition from numerous cardinals, St. Catherine persuaded Pope Gregory XI to return to Rome in 1377 to restore order. The papacy had resided in Avignon for much of that century.*

JOAN OF ARC (1412–1431)

FEAST DAY:	*May 30*
SYMBOLS IN ART:	*None known*
PATRONAGE:	*France*
PAINTINGS:	*Ingres, Dominic,* Joan d'Arc
PROFILE:	*French mystic, soldier, and martyr, whose real name was Jeanne la Pucelle*

T HE MAID OF ORLÉANS lived during the Hundred Years War waged by England and France, and for a few months this peasant girl became the toast of the French crown. Her rise to power was as swift as her fall. No other saint can claim to have achieved such fame and infamy in so short a life, ending as it did before her twentieth birthday.

"SAVE FRANCE!"

With France embroiled in civil war, the door was open for Henry V of England to invade Normandy. Defeat at the Battle of Agincourt and the subsequent conquest by the English armies of numerous cities shattered French morale.

It was in her fourteenth year that Joan (the English name for Jeanne), started to hear "voices" telling her to save France. She gradually identified the speakers as Saints Michael, Catherine of Alexandria, and Margaret of Antioch. But their messages were oblique. When, in obedience to them, she presented herself dressed for battle to the commander of the king's forces, she was laughed out of court. However, her premonition of a heavy French defeat persuaded the commander to think again, and she was referred to the dauphin (son of the deceased king), Charles. When a council of theologians could find nothing wrong with her and suggested the king make use of her services, Joan's whirlwind military campaign began.

FROM SOLDIER TO WITCH

Clad in white armor and bearing a special flag denoting Christian protection, the adolescent head of the French army entered the besieged town of Orléans. Her charismatic presence so boosted morale that within ten days the English forts surrounding the town had been captured. Further military successes followed until the way was clear for the dauphin to be crowned King Charles VII, with Joan standing proudly beside him holding her banner of God.

The "voices" had been vindicated—France had repelled the invader. But the king—and Joan—still had enemies at home. A military blunder left the young heroine at the mercy of the Duke of Burgundy, whose prisoner she became.

Having no use for her, the duke sold Joan to her erstwhile enemy, the English, knowing that to do so would bring certain death. The Church attributed her success to witchcraft and put her on trial. She was declared a heretic and handed over to the secular authorities, who burned her at the stake in the marketplace in Rouen (English territory).

Twenty years after her death, Joan's family asked for a retrial and a papal commission pronounced her innocent. She is venerated as a national heroine who endured persecution and death for the sake of her belief that she had acted on God's command. She was canonized in 1920.

ABOVE *Joan of Arc at the coronation of Charles VII. Painted by Ingres.*

POPE PIUS X (1835–1914)

FEAST DAY:	*August 21*
SYMBOLS IN ART:	*None*
PATRONAGE:	*Holy Communion*
PAINTINGS:	*None known*
PROFILE:	*Conservative Italian pope who endeavored to prevent World War I*

THE HISTORIAN OF POPES, Baron von Pastor, said of Pius X, "He was one of those chosen few men whose personality is irresistible. Everyone was moved by his simplicity and his angelic kindness … all who were ever admitted to his presence had a deep conviction of being face to face with a saint." Pius X is the last pope to have been canonized in over 400 years.

From the outset of his pontificate, Pius X (christened Giuseppe Sarto) made it clear that he wished to be a religious rather than a political pope. His vow that he was born poor, would live poor, and would die poor gave his office an uncharacteristic humility. He disliked the wealth and ceremony of the Vatican, and used his authority to promote Catholic social work, especially among the poor indigenous people of Latin America. He even asked his clergy to make large material sacrifices so that the Church in France could become independent of an overbearing government.

Pius was a man of great principle and little compromise. Many remember him for his dogmatic stand against modernizing tendencies, both within the Roman Catholic Church and in society generally. He refused to engage in ecumenical dialogue between the churches, and condemned materialistic greed and egalitarian political systems, such as communism and socialism. He considered most forms of rule by the people undesirable, including democracy, and instead he encouraged people to spend more time servicing their faith by, for example, taking Holy Communion on a daily basis.

IMPENDING WAR

What set Pius apart from his contemporaries was his spiritual awareness of the state of the world and its blind march into the catastrophe of 1914. "Truly we are passing through disastrous times when we may well make our own the lamentation of the prophet: 'There is no truth and there is no mercy, and there is no knowledge of God in the land' (Hosea 4:1)." Despite his tireless efforts to avert the crisis, Pius remained helpless on August 4 of that year—the anniversary of his election to the Holy See—as the nations of Europe went to war. The outbreak of World War I is said to have killed him. He developed bronchitis and died on August 19, 1914.

Several acclaimed miracles were reported close to the time of his death, both before and after it. Although Pius X had his critics, the voice was unanimous on his holiness, and the process of beatification began in 1923, ending with his canonization in 1954.

ABOVE *Pius X at the start of his pontificate in 1903.*

ABOVE *Newspapers acknowledged a pope who was alive to new developments.*

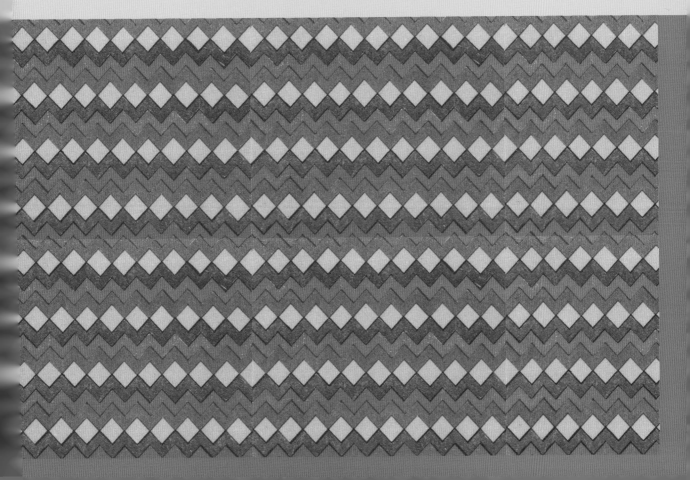

CHAPTER 6

SUFFERING

JOHN THE BAPTIST (FIRST CENTURY)

FEAST DAY:	*June 24 (birth); August 29 (death)*
SYMBOLS IN ART:	*Lamb, cross, honeycomb, ax, pelt tunic*
PATRONAGE:	*Epileptics, convulsive children, bird dealers, farriers, tailors*
PAINTINGS:	*Bruegel, Pieter,* The Sermon of St. John the Baptist; *Caravaggio,* St. John the Baptist; *del Sarto, Andrea,* John the Baptist; *da Vinci, Leonardo,* St. John the Baptist
PROFILE:	*Biblical prophet who baptized Jesus as the new Messiah; his birth to Elizabeth, cousin of the Virgin Mary, was foretold to his father Zachariah, a temple priest*

MIDSUMMER'S DAY

St. John's feast day falls unusually on the anniversary not of his death but of his birth, which is also Midsummer's Day. On St. John's Eve, bonfires traditionally were lit, supposedly to strengthen the Sun, which then begins to recede into winter.

MUCH MYSTERY surrounds the New Testament story of John the Baptist. A wild figure, dressed in camel hair and said to live on plants, emerges from the Judaean Desert calling everyone to repentance. His singling out of one man, Jesus, as the expected Messiah, who in turn recognizes John as the greatest of the Hebrew prophets, has led some scholars to believe they were close friends. They may even have belonged to the same ascetic group, such as the Qumran community, whose monastery ruins are located a short distance from where John performed baptisms in the River Jordan.

REVIVALIST PREACHER OR MESSIANIC FIGURE?

There were probably many religious groups in Palestine preaching the coming of the end of time. In preparation, some urged a return to traditional spiritual values, while others wished for an active rebellion against the Roman occupiers of their country. John was clearly feared by the nominal Jewish king, who owed his authority to Caesar. After the scene of mass baptism, John disappears from the Gospel narrative only to reappear as a prisoner of the Jewish ruler Herod Antipas, no doubt perceived as a threat to the existing order.

It is possible that John led a rival movement alongside the early Church. He may even have claimed to be a messiah himself. Certainly some of the Gospels regarded him as being the Old Testament prophet Elijah, who was expected to return to the world in a messianic role. It is speculated that Jesus and John may have led two competing messianic movements.

SALOME'S DANCE OF DEATH

John became a victim of his own outspoken courage. He was imprisoned in the palace of Machaerus beside the Dead Sea for denouncing the incestuous union of Herod with his niece and brother's wife, Herodias. Her hatred for John led to the instigation of her daughter Salome's dance before the impressionable Herod, who was so beguiled that he offered her anything she wished. Prompted by her mother, she demanded John's head. Within minutes the executioner's deed was done and the severed head was brought to the banquet hall on a silver platter.

ABOVE *A 13th-century Armenian manuscript illumination of the baptism of Jesus.*

STEPHEN (DIED C. 35)

FEAST DAY:	*December 26*
SYMBOLS IN ART:	*Stones, palm of martyrdom*
PATRONAGE:	*Headaches, deacons, horses*
PAINTINGS:	*Carpaccio, Vittore,* Disputation of St. Stephen; *di Bondone, Giotto,* St. Stephen; *Rubens,* The Martyrdom of St. Stephen; *Uccello, Paolo,* Stoning of St. Stephen
PROFILE:	*First Christian martyr*

ABOVE *As the persecutors of St. Stephen hurled stones against him he prayed that their sin should not be held against them.*

T
HE FIRST MARTYRDOM of a Christian—a good nine years before that of any apostle—must have been a sobering moment for the followers of the new faith. In the first few years after Christ's death they constituted no more than a radical group within Judaism, and as such were up against the full force of the religious establishment. Jealously guarding their authority, the Jewish elders treated any claim to messiahship with such neurotic suspicion that it was likely to result in a charge of blasphemy, an offense punishable by death. Such was the fate of Stephen, whose preaching so angered the Jews that he was dragged through the streets of Jerusalem and stoned to death outside the gates.

WHY STEPHEN, NOT AN APOSTLE?

Stephen's eloquent address in the Acts of the Apostles in the New Testament condemns the Jews for killing Christ, whom, he bravely declares, God had sent to supersede the Law of Moses and temple worship. These words would have struck deep into Jewish hearts—even some Jewish Christians did not yet accept that a new age of the Holy Spirit had dawned. At this time Jerusalem had an ethnically mixed population: Native Hebrews often clashed with foreign Hellenists (Greek-speakers). While converts to Christianity naturally came from both sectors, the apostles tended to be more traditional, whereas Stephen and others were Hellenists with a modern, radical outlook.

When the Jewish authorities unleashed the first wave of persecution against the Church, it was Stephen, a leader of this Hellenist wing, who suffered most. This explains why many Christians fled to the safer region of Samaria, while the apostles stayed in Jerusalem.

Stephen's position in the Church was as one of the seven deacons elected to carry out administrative tasks, which the apostles did not have time to do themselves. The deacons provided a sort of local welfare service. Stephen's task was to ensure that enough food reached Christian widows in Jerusalem, especially in his own Greek-speaking community.

FEAST DAY CUSTOM

In honor of the saint's martyrdom in Poland, people celebrate St. Stephen's Day by throwing oats at the priest after Mass in imitation of the act of stoning. The custom is also linked to an ancient fertility rite in which Polish boys and girls cast walnuts at each other on this day.

PETER (DIED C. 64)

FEAST DAY:	*June 29 (shared with St. Paul)*
SYMBOLS IN ART:	*Keys, ship, fish, cockerel*
PATRONAGE:	*Church and papacy*
PAINTINGS:	*Bosch, Hieronymus,* The St. Peter with the Donor; *Caravaggio,* The Denial of St. Peter; *El Greco,* Apostle St. Peter; *Rembrandt,* Peter Denouncing Christ
PROFILE:	*Fisherman and leader of the apostles; two New Testament epistles ascribed to him*

ROMAN PERSECUTIONS OF CHRISTIANS

❖

NERO, 64 C.E.: Christians made scapegoats for the fire of Rome

DOMITIAN, 95 C.E.: Executions and banishment from the empire

TRAJAN, 112 C.E.: Trials of Christians in Bithynia (Asia Minor)

AURELIUS, 177 C.E.: Severe persecution in Lyons

DECIUS, 250 C.E.: Systematic attack on the Church by insistence on the worship of pagan gods of the state

DIOCLETIAN, 303 C.E.: Churches destroyed and bibles burned; later executions

THE SAINT MOST VENERATED in the Roman Catholic Church was the disciple Jesus called the "rock" on which the Church should be built. He was well known for his weaknesses—impetuousness, inconstancy, timidity—and no one was more surprised at the choice than Peter himself, who was reluctant to accept the role. Yet, come the Day of Pentecost, he was apparently transformed by the power of the Holy Spirit to pioneer the new faith and become a source of strength to his brethren.

DISCIPLESHIP

By all accounts (Mark's Gospel is based on Peter's memoir), the Galilean fisherman was a modest man, married and God-fearing. He was probably happy to lead a quiet life. He became a privileged witness to certain special events in Jesus's ministry: The Transfiguration, the raising of Jairus's daughter, and Jesus's agony in the Garden of Gethsemane.

On other occasions his character is tested. His attempt to emulate Jesus's walking on the lake fails when his faith falters; the candid "confession," on the other hand, that Jesus is the awaited Messiah shows his insight; and the enthusiastic rush to see the empty tomb indicates his devotion. Despite his three denials after the cock had crowed of being a follower of Jesus, Peter is given the "keys of the kingdom of Heaven," a phrase used by the later Church as confirmation of Peter's primacy among the apostles.

AS APOSTLE FOR CHRIST

After Pentecost, Peter takes the lead in the early Church in Jerusalem. Miraculous cures are attributed to him, and according to scripture, he escapes from prison by angelic intervention. In baptizing the Roman centurion Cornelius, Peter is the first to extend salvation to the Gentiles, who, in not being among God's chosen people, were traditionally excluded from redemption.

Well-attested tradition makes Peter the first bishop of Rome, hence its papal seat. And it was here that he is supposed to have been martyred during the reign of Nero. Peter was one of several Christians, possibly including St. Paul, who were living in the capital of the empire and were falsely blamed for the fire of Rome in 64 C.E. On receiving his sentence of death by crucifixion, Peter is said to have asked to be hung upside down.

ABOVE *In El Greco's depiction of St. Peter repenting for his denial of Christ, the possessor of the keys to Heaven is blessed with a glimpse of Paradise.*

JUDE (FIRST CENTURY)

FEAST DAY: *October 28*

SYMBOLS IN ART: *Club, ship, sword*

PATRONAGE: *Lost causes; desperate people*

PAINTINGS: *Cranach, Lucas the Elder,* Apostles Thaddaeus and Simon; *Dyck, Anthonis van,* The Apostle Judas Thaddaeus; *El Greco,* Apostle St. Thaddeus (Jude)

PROFILE: *Apostle and martyr; also called Judas (not Iscariot) or Thaddaeus, brother of James the Less; author of New Testament Epistle*

WHEN ALL SEEMS hopelessly lost, a prayer to St. Jude may help. Although little is known of him besides the instances arising in the New Testament and the epistle that he is dubiously credited with writing, few other saints are called upon quite so often for their intercession. Hardly a day goes by without some individual expressing his or her desperation to the saint in the personal columns of assorted newspapers. In fact, he has become an iconic figure of distress and failure for life in the modern world—the British novelist Thomas Hardy named his tragic central character after him in *Jude the Obscure*.

However seriously St. Jude's cause may be taken, it is said that the origin of his patronage lies in no greater achievement on his part than having a name resembling that of Judas Iscariot, the betrayer of Christ. For this reason nobody wished to invoke his name, and so he is prepared to support even the most desperate of his petitioners' predicaments.

REVOLUTIONARY ZEALOT?
The apocryphal document entitled "The Passion of Simon and Jude" is the main source of information about Jude outside the New Testament. It describes the preaching and martyrdom of the two apostles in Persia. It is thought that, because Jude's companion on these travels in Asia was Simon the Zealot, Jude may himself have been a zealot (Jewish militant nationalist of first-century Israel). He is sometimes depicted in art brandishing a sword, which may point to this role. Elsewhere he is shown with a club, the implement by which he suffered martyrdom, and a ship to symbolize his missionary endeavors.

BEARER OF THE TURIN SHROUD?

Tradition says the burial cloth in which Jesus was wrapped, later speculated to be the Shroud of Turin, was taken from the empty tomb by Thaddaeus, thought to be the same person as Jude. He is said to have brought it to Edessa, now Urfa, in Turkey. A shroud bearing the image of Christ, called the "Mandylion," was discovered there in the sixth century and moved to Constantinople. After Crusaders sacked the city in 1204, the cloth disappeared and is thought to have been smuggled to France, where it was safeguarded until it was later enshrined in Turin Cathedral.

ABOVE *St. Jude, by the Flemish master Van Dyck (1599–1641), has become a modern icon of failure.*

See also RITA OF CASCIA *page 118*

IGNATIUS OF ANTIOCH (DIED C. 107)

FEAST DAY:	*October 17*
SYMBOLS IN ART:	*Chains, lions*
PATRONAGE:	*Throat diseases*
PAINTINGS:	*None known*
PROFILE:	*Bishop of Antioch in Syria, and martyr*

ONE OF THE EARLIEST Church fathers, who was probably a disciple of Saints Peter and Paul, is best known for his letters written in the last months of his life while traveling under arrest from Antioch to Rome. Little of his ministry as a bishop is documented, but tradition regards Ignatius as an important figure of the early Church. His letters show an ardent devotion to Christ and belief in the Resurrection. In a grand gesture of self-sacrifice he referred to himself as the "bearer of God," whom he longed to meet.

THE FINAL JOURNEY

Clearly, this final passage of his life prepared him spiritually for the coming ordeal. Having confessed to being a Christian, he was arrested during the Trajan persecution, which ripped through Christian communities in the Roman Empire at the beginning of the second century. His journey to Rome was taking him to his arena of death, probably the Colisseum, where he would be thrown to the lions in the imperial games.

A letter to the Church there shows that he fully embraced the idea of martyrdom for Christ's sake and did not wish anyone to intercede on his behalf:

ABOVE *Roman centurions lead St. Ignatius, bishop of Antioch, to his fate in the Colisseum of ancient Rome.*

> *I die for Christ of my own choice, unless you hinder me. I beseech you not to show "inopportune kindness" to me [a Greek proverb says "inopportune kindness is as bad as enmity"]. Let me be given to the wild beasts, for by their means I can attain to God. I am God's wheat, and I am being ground by the teeth of the beasts so that I may appear as pure bread.*

Indeed, Ignatius seems to relish the manner of his imminent death:

> *Let all come, fire and cross and conflicts with beasts, hacking, cutting, wrenching of bones, chopping of limbs, the crushing of my body, cruel chastisements of the devil laid upon me. Only let me attain to Jesus Christ.* [*]

On the way to his fate, Ignatius says he learned to "abandon all desire" as his spirit readied itself for its fulfillment. "There is not in me any sensuous fire," he added; even food had lost its taste.

[*] H. Bettenson, *The Early Christian Fathers.*

SEBASTIAN (DIED C. 303)

FEAST DAY: *January 20*
SYMBOLS IN ART: *Arrows*
PATRONAGE: *Protector against epidemics (especially plague); archers, athletes, soldiers*
PAINTINGS: *Botticelli, St. Sebastian; H. Holbein, Martyrdom of St. Sebastian;*
School of Caravaggio, St. Sebastian; School of A. Dürer, Young Man as St. Sebastian
PROFILE: *Roman soldier and martyr*

RENAISSANCE LEGACY

❖

The earliest pictures of Sebastian are Ravenna mosaics in which he is represented as an old man. His popularity took a new turn in Renaissance Italy, when his martyrdom became a source of artistic expression for such painters as Bernini, Botticelli, and El Greco. He was usually depicted as an effeminate male nude, transfixed with arrows, and he has been adopted unofficially as a gay icon, for example, in Derek Jarman's film *Sebastian*

A ROMAN SOLDIER became one of the best known of the early martyrs by virtue of his later popularity with Renaissance painters. Little is known about him, except that he is thought to have suffered in Emperor Diocletian's persecution and was buried along the Appian Way in Rome.

TRADITION OF HIS MARTYRDOM
A fifth-century legend recounts how he joined the Roman army and became a captain under Diocletian. When it was discovered that he was a Christian and had converted many others, he was ordered to be shot with arrows. His executioners left him for dead but a Christian widow found him alive and nursed him back to health. In a courageous act of duty, he reported back to Diocletian, who promptly ordered him to be beaten to death. His body was found in a sewer and taken to the catacombs for burial outside of Rome. His capacity for physical endurance led to his adoption by athletes as their patron saint.

PROTECTOR AGAINST EPIDEMICS
Sebastian's patronage against epidemics possibly stems from the association of arrows with disease (in Roman mythology, the god Apollo's arrows led to illness). The fact that he recovered from their infliction, which resembles the eruption of the skin caused by the plague, suggested his immunity from such epidemics.
Traditions of his valiant intercession on behalf of cities beset with pestilence abound in medieval legends. In 680, his patronage freed Rome from a raging fever; likewise Milan and Lisbon in the sixteenth century.

ABOVE *A costume design of 1911 on the theme of St. Sebastian's martyrdom, painted by Leon Bakst.*

See also GEORGE *page 94,* MARTIN OF TOURS *page 137*

CATHERINE OF ALEXANDRIA (4TH CENTURY*)

FEAST DAY:	*November 25 (formerly)*
SYMBOLS IN ART:	*Spiked wheel*
PATRONAGE:	*Craftsmen who work with a wheel (potters, spinners), teachers, lawyers, philosophers, unmarried girls, the dying*
PAINTINGS:	*Raphael, St. Catherine of Alexandria*
PROFILE:	*Legendary martyr; one of the Fourteen Holy Helpers; reduced cult status in 1969*

ONE OF THE MOST POPULAR SAINTS in Europe during the Middle Ages has more legend about her than fact. Her cult emerged in the ninth century at the foot of Mt. Sinai, where a monastery dedicated to her was founded on the legend that her body was taken there by "angels" (a term sometimes used to refer to monks).

The further tradition of her life tells of a learned girl of noble birth in Alexandria. She complained about the enforced worship of idols to Emperor Maxentius, who called in 50 philosophers to refute her argument. But it was she who refuted them, and they were put to death for their failure. On being ordered to denounce her Christian faith, she refused. Furthermore, when she turned down the emperor's offer of marriage, she was beaten for two hours before being thrown into prison.

THE CATHERINE WHEEL

While confined to her cell she is said to have been fed by a dove and that Christ appeared to her in a vision. Her visitors in prison included the empress, who, curious to see such an extraordinary young girl, became so touched by her words that she too converted and was put to death. Catherine's Christian influence, even in jail, was sufficient to worry the emperor, and he tried to have her broken on a wheel. With her hands and feet tied to a spiked wheel, she was about to be rotated when the structure split and fell apart. The spectacle of flying splinters, which were supposed to have killed bystanders, forms the basis for the Catherine wheel, the firecracker used in celebrations today. The virgin martyr did not escape, however. A simpler, more effective method of execution was expedited by the use of a sword to cut off her head.

GUIDING LIGHT

In association with the saint's emblem of the spiked wheel, mechanics and wheelwrights placed themselves under her patronage. Before studying or writing, students and philosophers used to invoke her aid in guiding their pens to eloquent expression. The devotion to St. Catherine, which assumed such vast proportions in Europe after the Crusades, reached its apogee in France during the fifteenth century. It was said that she had appeared to Joan of Arc and, together with St. Michael, had been divinely appointed as Joan's adviser.

ABOVE *Catherine of Alexandria spurned marriage to the emperor because she was already "wedded to Christ."*

*date uncertain

ABOVE *Heated disputes between Henry II of England
and his archbishop Thomas à Becket became so
frequent that loyal servants to the realm took it upon
themselves to rid the king of the object of his despair.*

Thomas à Becket (1118–1170)

FEAST DAY: *December 29*
SYMBOLS IN ART: *Pallium, miter, and archbishop's cross, sword through skull*
PATRONAGE: *Clergy*
PAINTINGS: *None known*
PROFILE: *Archbishop of Canterbury martyred in his cathedral*

THE INSPIRATION behind Geoffrey Chaucer's epic medieval poem *Canterbury Tales* was Thomas à Becket's martyrdom, a horrific incident that turned Canterbury Cathedral into one of the most popular pilgrimage sites in Europe. Under the weight of great acclaim, with reports of miracles at his shrine running into many hundreds, the pope of the day had little choice but to canonize the priest whose life was taken in such a sacrilegious manner.

DUAL PERSONALITY

Though readily declared a saint by the religious authorities, Becket had made many enemies in his time. His personality does not fit the stereotype of an altruistic man of God. Imperious, ambitious, and even violent, he conducted his early life with little regard for pious devotion. Born in London of wealthy Norman parents, he became good friends with King Henry II and in 1155 was appointed chancellor of the realm. Outwardly, he gave all the appearances of enjoying a life indulging in extravagant worldliness in his role as diplomat and statesman, while remaining loyal to his king, whose army he even led into battle.

Yet all this gusto evaporated when Henry appointed him archbishop of Canterbury in 1162. He changed, as he himself admitted, from being "a patron of play-actors and follower of hounds, to being a shepherd of souls."* Gone was the lavish entertainment—in its place, austerity and dedication to the duties of his new office. Whereas Henry expected his friend to support him in curtailing the power of the Church, which was challenging his royal authority, Becket did the opposite and defended its rights.

"TURBULENT PRIEST"

After a quarrel over the jurisdiction of clergy convicted of crimes, the two men became bitter enemies and Becket was forced to live in France as an exile. Six years passed before they were reconciled, though only briefly, before they argued again, this time over the excommunication of bishops who had supported the king in Becket's absence. On hearing the news, a despairing Henry uttered the reckless words, "Who will rid me of this turbulent priest?" Four barons took him literally and set off for Canterbury. In a side chapel of the cathedral they committed the murder in cold blood. The whole of Christendom let out a collective howl in horror. The king, racked with guilt, gladly served three years of penance in contrition.

The story of Thomas à Becket has inspired several literary expressions, including Tennyson's dramatic poem *Becket*, T. S. Eliot's *Murder in the Cathedral*, and Jean Anouilh's play *Becket*, made into a film in 1964.

ABOVE *Murder in the cathedral.*

*D. Knowles,
Thomas Becket

RITA OF CASCIA (1381–1457)

FEAST DAY: *May 22*
SYMBOLS IN ART: *Wounded forehead*
PATRONAGE: *Desperate people, unhappy wives*
PAINTINGS: *Anonymous (see below)*
PROFILE: *Italian widow, Augustinian nun, and mystic*

LIKE ST. JUDE, Rita became a patron for those whose lives were filled with despair for their loved ones. Every year thousands of pilgrims, especially victims of marital abuse, visit her glass shrine to view her incorrupt body.

Rita's troubles began when, against her own desire to lead a religious life, she assented to her parents' wishes that she should marry. However, their choice was an unhappy one. Her husband proved to be alcoholic, violent, and unfaithful. For 18 years she suffered his attacks and infidelities, and, worse still, gradually saw her two sons fall under his influence. Eventually, one day, her husband fell victim to his own brutal world and was brought home to her dead, covered in wounds.

Her sons' vows to avenge his death only made her more sorrowful as she feared the consequences. In the depths of despair she resolved to pray that her sons might die before any murder was committed. In answer to her prayer, they both contracted a fatal disease before discovering the identity of their father's killer. With loving tenderness their mother nursed them through their sickness and succeeded in turning their minds to a Christian spirit of forgiveness before their deaths.

THE SUFFERING OF A MYSTIC

Alone in the world, Rita returned to the idea of joining a nunnery. Although the rules forbade entry to any but virgins, her persistent applications to the convent of Augustinian nuns at Cascia eventually persuaded the mother superior to grant her admittance in 1413. The same selfless devotion she had shown to her family she now expressed to her religious sisters, especially in her care for them in times of illness.

Even as a child she had a special sympathy with the sufferings of Christ. One day, nearly 30 years after joining the convent, Rita experienced a sense of mystical union with Christ during a sermon on the crown of thorns. While kneeling in prayer, she became aware of a pain in her head, as though a thorn from the crucifix had lodged itself in her forehead. A suppurating wound developed and became so offensive to the other nuns that she was kept in almost constant seclusion until her death from tuberculosis 16 years later.

Her reputation for holiness and for providing comfort to those in need has made her a popular saint today, especially in Italy. Her patronage of desperate situations, in particular those involving matrimonial strife, keeps her services well in demand.

ABOVE *The pathos of St. Rita's devotion found its most acute expression in the sensation of a thorn lodged in her forehead as she contemplated the Passion of Christ. Painting by an anonymous 19th-century artist.*

See also JUDE *page 112*

JOHN OF GOD (1495–1550)

FEAST DAY:	*March 8*
SYMBOLS IN ART:	*Alms, crown of thorns, heart*
PATRONAGE:	*The sick, hospitals, nurses, heart patients, alcoholics, booksellers*
PAINTINGS:	*Horvath, Werner, St. John of God*
PROFILE:	*Portuguese mercenary and penitent; founder of the Hospitallers, Brothers of St. John of God*

F ROM MERCENARY KILLER to nurse of the dying, this man, like few other saints, experienced life's moral gamut. An unprincipled young man, whose family name is not known, he left home to earn his way as a member of a tough mercenary corps fighting for the Spanish crown. On the troop's disbandment he took whatever work was available—shepherding in Andalusia, even selling slaves to the Moors in North Africa. Rootless and lacking direction, John reached the age of 40 with sorrow in his heart. As he reflected on his past, the first stirrings of the Catholic faith in which he was raised prompted him to question his values.

STRICKEN CONSCIENCE

He began to discern elements of the sacrificial life as a peddler of religious books, a job he did for virtually no profit. During this period he is said to have received a vision of the infant Jesus, who bestowed on him the unlikely name by which he came to be known, John of God. Following directions revealed in the vision, he eagerly traveled to Granada, where he met a famous priest, John of Avila.

This encounter precipitated a sort of mental breakdown. While listening to the preacher's sermon in church, John of God suddenly began shouting and weeping, apparently in leave of his senses. He tore through the streets like a madman and had to be forcibly subdued into the local asylum. After several months of recuperation and counseling from John of Avila, who recognized the signs of remorse, John recovered his senses and was a changed man. He embarked on a new course for which the entire region would later praise his endeavors.

THE POOR HOUSE

To make up for the misery he had caused as a soldier, John rented a house in Granada and opened it to anyone in need of help. A letter he wrote describes the task he undertook:

So many poor people come here that I very often wonder how we can care for them all … More than a hundred and ten are now living here … Since this house is open to everyone, it receives the sick of every type and condition: the crippled, the disabled, lepers, mutes, the insane, paralytics, those suffering from scurvy and those bearing the afflictions of old age, many children, and above all countless pilgrims and travelers … I work here on borrowed money, a prisoner for the sake of Jesus Christ. And often my debts are so pressing that I dare not go out of the house for fear of being seized by my creditors. Whenever I see so many poor brothers and neighbors of mine suffering beyond their strength and overwhelmed with so many ills which I cannot alleviate, then I become exceedingly sorrowful; but I trust in Christ, who knows my heart.

What John began in this humble way became the foundation for a hospitalers charity instituted after his death, called Brothers of St. John of God. As a result he was made patron of hospitals and the sick.

ABOVE *Once an outsider himself, St. John opened his heart and home to those less fortunate.*

TERESA OF AVILA (1515–1582)

FEAST DAY:	*October 15*
SYMBOLS IN ART:	*Fiery arrow, dove*
PATRONAGE:	*Protector against illness, headaches, people ridiculed for their piety, Spain*
PAINTINGS:	*Blanchet, Thomas,* St. Teresa of Avila; *Cagnacci, Guido,* St. Teresa of Avila Before the Cross; *de la Miseria, Fray Juan,* St. Teresa of Avila
PROFILE:	*Founder of the reformed order of the Discalced Carmelites; first woman saint to be made a Doctor of the Church, in 1970*

No CHRISTIAN MYSTIC had a greater impact on the religious life of sixteenth-century Spain than did Teresa of Avila. Her intense search for union with God coupled with remarkable energy and business acumen revolutionized the contemplative life, inspiring generations of women and men.

Born of aristocratic parentage in Avila, near Madrid, Teresa was a spirited and gifted girl with an avid interest in the fashion of Castilian Spain. However, repeated illness in her youth set her back and, on reading the letters of St. Jerome, she stunned her family and admirers by deciding, at the age of 20, that she wished to join a Carmelite convent.

SEARCH FOR AUSTERITY

Soon after taking her vows, Teresa became seriously ill. Medical help was limited and she never fully recovered her health. She began receiving heavenly visions, which Dominican and Jesuit examiners pronounced to be divine. Over the next 20 years her contemplative life deepened and she desired a more austere rule than that followed by contemporary Carmelites. There was too much comfort, too many possessions, and too much contact with the outside world.

In a bid to return to the austere poverty characteristic of the twelfth-century rule originated in Palestine, Teresa used her family wealth to found a reformed convent in Avila, which became known as the Discalced (meaning "unshod") Carmelites. She traveled the length and breadth of Spain preaching the reformed model and opened another 16 convents. With her companion John of the Cross, who led similar reforms in monasteries, she posed a formidable threat to the existing order and aroused much opposition from church authorities.

THE SWEET PAIN OF DIVINE LOVE

Teresa's prolific writings include her *Life*, an uninhibited, unstructured autobiography, considered to be the feminine equivalent of St. Augustine's *Confessions*. In it she describes her mystical experiences. The high point was an ecstasy (famously, though oversensually, represented in a sculpture by Bernini), in which an angel appeared to her carrying a spear tipped with the fire of divine love. On being plunged into her heart, the spear infused her innermost self. She describes a sensation both of intense pain and ineffable sweetness, representing the exquisite union of the believer with God. Other writings include *The Interior Castle* and *The Way of Perfection*.

> *"Let everyone understand that real love of God does not consist in tear-shedding, nor in that sweetness and tenderness for which we usually long, just because they console us, but in serving God in justice, fortitude of soul and humility."* From St. Teresa's *Life*.

The Interior Castle was written in 1577 to replace her autobiography, which had been confiscated by the Inquisition. It describes the mystical life by presenting an allegory of the growth of the soul through prayer toward union with God. The castle is the soul, its keeper is God dwelling within it. The life of prayer is a progression through the rooms of the castle from the dark outer ring to the light in the center.

See also JOHN OF THE CROSS *page 122*

ABOVE *Expressions of St. Teresa's religious ecstasy
became a popular subject for patrons of the arts who
aspired to capture the intensity of her faith.*

JOHN OF THE CROSS (1542–1591)

FEAST DAY:	*December 14*
SYMBOLS IN ART:	*None*
PATRONAGE:	*Mystics, Spanish poets*
PAINTINGS:	*Lorenzetti, Pietro,* Pope Honorius III Approves the Carmelite Order
PROFILE:	*Spanish poet and mystical theologian; virtual co-founder of the Discalced Carmelite friars; made a Doctor of the Church in 1926*

ABOVE *The reform of the Carmelite Order, here receiving its papal blessing, reflected the uncompromising purity of spirit which St. John of the Cross expressed in his poetry.*

I IS SAID that with John of the Cross the mystical tradition in Christianity "touched one of its rare summits,"* that his lyrical purity lifts the heart nearer to God than do the writings of any other saint. Born in Avila, near Madrid, to a good family living in reduced circumstances, John joined the Carmelite friars and studied theology at Salamanca University. A meeting with Teresa of Avila convinced him of the true way of sanctity through her reforming ideals and he supported her in founding the Discalced ("unshod") Carmelite houses.

The appeal of their reforms, which emphasized austerity and simplicity of devotion in pursuit of greater union with God, spread throughout Catholic Spain. But with the star of Protestantism rising elsewhere in Europe, the Roman Catholic Church wished to discourage a faith of personal mysticism with its implications for their authority.

THE DARK NIGHT

Fearing that this mystic's influence might turn out to be as great on Spain as Martin Luther's was on Germany, the Church endeavored to stamp out the religious "rebellion" by persecuting its leaders. John of the Cross was captured and incarcerated in the unreformed (Calced) Carmelite monastery of Toledo in 1575. In an age when the Inquisition resorted to brutal methods to deter heresy, the treatment meted out to him was as harsh as was the determination to correct his error. The unrelenting friar was confined to a tiny, dark cell, bitterly cold in winter and unbearably hot in summer. The foul-smelling air, poor food, and dysentery drained his health and spirit; at times he prayed for his death. Most crushing of all was the growing sense of his abandonment by God.

Spiritually alone and filled with anguish, John was in the depths of despair when a change of fortune came his way. A new jailer took pity on him and improved his conditions so much that John felt his life renewed. The depredations he had suffered became the inspiration for poetic works about the mystical journey of the soul to God, notably in *The Dark Night of the Soul.* Other works include *The Ascent of Mount Carmel, The Canticle of the Spirit,* and *The Living Flame of Love.*

After nine months in prison John escaped with the help of his lenient jailer. He devoted the rest of his life to running the Discalced Carmelite Order, which separated soon afterward from the unreformed Calceds.

*O. Chadwick,
The Reformation.*

See also TERESA OF AVILA *page 120*

BERNADETTE OF LOURDES (1844–1879)

FEAST DAY:	*April 16*
SYMBOLS IN ART:	*None*
PATRONAGE:	*Mortal and chronic sickness, poverty, shepherds*
PAINTINGS:	*None known*
PROFILE:	*French visionary*

T HE GREATEST Christian shrine today lies in the foothills of the Pyrenees in France, where a young sickly girl is said to have experienced a series of visions of the Virgin Mary. Subsequently, she become the instrument of many miraculous cures.

VISIONS AND MIRACULOUS CURES

Marie Bernard Soubirous, or Bernadette, as she became known, was an illiterate and asthmatic daughter of a miller in the small town of Lourdes. On February 11, 1858, at the age of 14, she was gathering firewood beside the River Gave when she saw a vision of a beautiful young woman at the mouth of a cave on the opposite side of the river. Between that date and July 16, she is said to have experienced 17 further apparitions of this figure, who eventually identified herself as the Virgin Mary, under the title of "the Immaculate Conception."

Many of these apparitions took place in the presence of other people but none could see or hear the Virgin. Bernadette uttered the Virgin's messages, exhorting people to be penitent and to pray for world peace. She also requested that a church be built in memory of these apparitions.

During one of Bernadette's visions, a spring at the mouth of the cave turned into a flowing stream which, to this day, is held to contain curative properties. Seven miraculous cures were reported that year, including the restoration of one man's sight and the healing of paralysis. Altogether, the Roman Catholic Church has recognized 65 miraculous cures in the name of Bernadette.

SUSPICION AND MALICE

Once Bernadette's visions had ceased, she was subjected to a series of intense interrogations by the Church and state officials. Numerous false visionaries emerged too, and suspicion grew about the whole phenomenon of apparitions. Bernadette, a simple half-witted girl, suffered from the insensitivity and meanness of others, though she bore the abuse with patience and fortitude. In 1866 she was admitted to the convent of the Sisters of Charity at Nevers. Although she was now sheltered from public malice, she suffered instead from the jealousy of her superiors.

Bernadette remained at the convent for the rest of her short life, succumbing to her sickly afflictions at the age of thirty-five. In 1909 her body was exhumed and found to be incorrupt. She was canonized in 1933, not for her visions and trances, but for her humility and trust in the religious faith that characterized her whole life.

ABOVE *Devotion to this poor, illiterate girl from 19th-century France is as great now as it has ever been.*

MAXIMILIAN KOLBE (1894–1941)

FEAST DAY:	*August 14*
SYMBOLS IN ART:	*None*
PATRONAGE:	*Political prisoners, drug addicts, families, journalists*
PAINTINGS:	*None*
PROFILE:	*Polish Franciscan priest and martyr at Auschwitz concentration camp*

ABOVE *The statue at Westminster Abbey in London commemorating Maximilian Kolbe's sacrifice.*

MAXIMILIAN KOLBE came from a background of patriotic resistance. His father was hung by the Russians in 1914 for opposing their occupation of his country, Poland. Like his father, Maximilian became a Franciscan friar and followed his example in standing up for national independence.

In 1936 he was made superior of Niepokalanow monastery, which housed more than 700 friars. Despite suffering recurrent bouts of tuberculosis, Maximilian poured his energies into fighting the rise of Nazism through militant journalism. Believing that Christian apathy would allow totalitarian regimes, both in Germany and the Soviet Union, to overrun Christian Europe, he strove to galvanize Christians to act on their principles. With the help of his fellow brethren he founded a weekly journal of Christian discourses and news.

After the German invasion of Poland brought about the closure of his monastery and its conversion to a refugee camp, Kolbe continued to turn out his journal, unafraid of criticizing the Third Reich or speaking out for independence. He refused German citizenship and was eventually arrested as an "intellectual" in 1941.

INTERNMENT AT AUSCHWITZ

Kolbe was forced to do hard labor, moving logs at speed and being beaten when tiring. Despite the extreme conditions he kept up morale and maintained his priestly duties by smuggling in bread and wine to celebrate Mass.

Attempts to escape from the camp were punished in a way known to all internees. Men from the same bunker as the escapees would be randomly selected for death by starvation. Following one such attempt, all prisoners from the particular bunker were paraded in preparation for the death sentences. One man from each line would have to die.

When the sentence was delivered to a captured Polish sergeant who had a wife and two children, Kolbe stepped forward and asked to take his place. The Nazi officer accepted the request and sent him, together with nine others, to the death chamber. An assistant to the janitor recorded for posterity Kolbe's peaceful demeanor, of how he continued his priestly function in preparing his fellow victims for death by saying prayers and psalms, which, by the end, were whispered for lack of strength. One by one they died until the only survivor was Kolbe, who was then administered a lethal injection.

In 1982 the Polish pope, John Paul II, whose former diocese of Cracow included Auschwitz, canonized Maximilian Kolbe. Present at the ceremony was the Polish sergeant whose life he had saved.

PADRE PIO (1887–1968)

FEAST DAY:	*September 23 (proposed)*
SYMBOLS IN ART:	*None*
PATRONAGE:	*None*
PAINTINGS:	*None*
PROFILE:	*Italian Capuchin friar and stigmatist; christened Francesco Forgione; canonized in 2002*

IN BEARING WOUNDS resembling those of the Crucifixion for 50 years, this Capuchin friar suffered the inexplicable phenomenon known as the stigmata of Christ longer than any other stigmatist in Christian history. What is more, Padre Pio bore the wounds gladly, believing their chronic pain to be the divine flames of love.

THE STIGMATA

Even as a boy he would rather pray than play. He entered the Capuchin Order, aged 15, and is said to have heard a voice telling him that he would be scourged and crucified like St. Francis, the first Christian stigmatist. On September 20, 1915, he felt the pains of the stigmata and exactly three years later, while kneeling before a crucifix, received the visible wounds on his hands, feet, and side of his chest. He describes the experience as a beautiful vision of Christ with rays of light transmitting the wounds to his body.

Thereafter they never ceased bleeding (shedding about a teacup of blood each day), nor did they ever heal or expand. He said the pain—at its worst during Eucharistic devotion—was like having nails driven into his body. The monk found the phenomenon embarrassing when he took Mass and wore white gloves to hide the disfigurements. Upon his death on September 23, 1968, the wounds disappeared, leaving the skin renewed and unblemished.

SPIRITUAL GIFTS

Padre Pio manifested other signs of divine presence. Accompanying the wounds was a specially fragrant odor similar to the scent of flowers. He was able to see into the hearts of penitents, who came to him in the thousands to utter their confessions, which he would hear for 10 or 12 hours every day. He was also famous for bilocation, the gift of being seen in a place other than where his physical body stood. The most celebrated occasion of this occurred during World War II, when Allied bombers targeted the little town of San Giovanni Rotondo, where it was thought a cache of Nazi weapons was hidden. The town happened to be the very one in which Padre Pio's friary was located. Successive missions reported seeing a monk whose description matched that of Padre Pio, flying in the sky and preventing pilots from entering the airspace. The surrounding area was obliterated but not one bomb fell on the town.

ABOVE *With a huge following world-wide, Padre Pio is one of Italy's most popular saints in modern times.*

MENINGITIS CURE

His canonization miracle involved the healing of a boy suffering from advanced meningitis in the House for Relief of Suffering, the hospital founded by Padre Pio. A prayer vigil attended by the boy's mother and Capuchin friars witnessed his sudden recovery after doctors had given up hope. The boy later claimed to have dreamed that night of a white-bearded monk who reassured him that he would recover.

See also FRANCIS OF ASSISI *page 38*

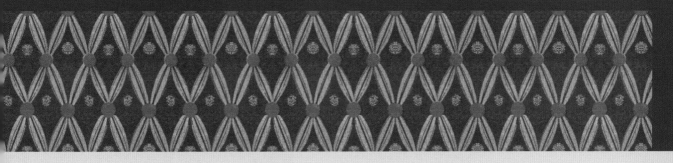

CHAPTER 7

PROFESSIONS AND OCCUPATIONS

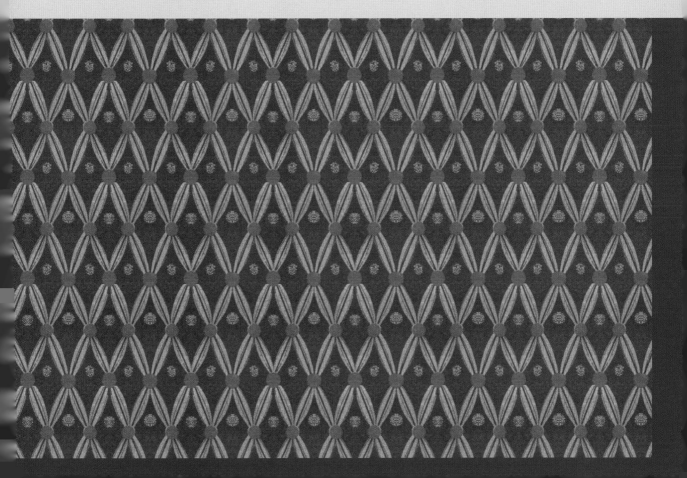

MATTHEW (FIRST CENTURY)

FEAST DAY:	*September 21*
SYMBOLS IN ART:	*Man with wings, bags of money, sword*
PATRONAGE:	*Accountants, bankers, and professionals connected with finance*
PAINTINGS:	*Caravaggio,* The Martyrdom of St. Matthew; *Hals, Frans,* St. Matthew; *Rembrandt,* Evangelist Matthew; *Terbruggen, Hendrick,* The Calling of St. Matthew
PROFILE:	*Tax collector, apostle and evangelist; also known as Levi*

ABOVE *A Romantic version of the calling of St. Matthew.*

No JEW IN PALESTINE at the time of Jesus's ministry was thought less likely to become an apostle than Matthew. As a volunteer tax collector on behalf of the Romans, he was a traitor in Jewish eyes and bitterly hated by his compatriots.

TAXMAN AND TOWN PARIAH

Every day Matthew would have sat in his customs house in Capernaum, a Galilean village that lay on the main trading route between Egypt and Damascus. As well as exacting the highest rates of excise duty they could from traders, tax gatherers were notorious for lining their pockets through bribery and extortion. Their dishonesty, as well as their betrayal, put them on a par, according to Jewish law, with robbers, murderers, and "unclean beasts;" the pariahs of society. In short, Matthew was a man living a lie. Upon receiving the call to be a disciple of Jesus, all changed in an instant as he rose from his counting table and left behind his rich pickings. Matthew was by far the wealthiest of the apostles.

FIRST EVANGELIST

Another distinction that set him apart from the rest of the apostles was his ability to read and write. The one article he did not leave behind was his pen, and with it, tradition maintains, he wrote the Gospel according to St. Matthew. More than the others, Matthew's Gospel was written for Jewish readers. He asserts the link between the Old and the New Testaments by presenting Jesus's ministry as a fulfillment of prophecy. Although Mark's account was written earlier, Matthew's is more complete and is placed in the New Testament canon as the primary Gospel. As though close to his heart, the main thrust of his Gospel is toward the "lost sheep of Israel," the sinners who have fallen foul of the law.

Little is known about his later life and death. He was reputedly martyred with a sword, some say in Ethiopia, others say in Persia. In Christian art he is usually depicted writing at a desk, with an angel guiding his quill. Sometimes he wears spectacles in order to help him read the small columns of figures of his accounts.

ABOVE *The realistic portrayal of Christ summoning St. Matthew, by J.J. Tissot, is based on the painter's numerous trips to the Holy Land made after a mystical experience.*

ANDREW (FIRST CENTURY)

FEAST DAY:	*November 30*
SYMBOLS IN ART:	*Saltire cross, fishing net*
PATRONAGE:	*Fishermen, anglers, Scotland, Russia*
PAINTINGS:	*Caravaggio*, The Crucifixion of St. Andrew*; Fouquet, Jean*, Martyrdom of St. Andrew*; El Greco*, Apostle St. Andrew*; Tintoretto*, St. Jerome and St. Andrew
PROFILE:	*Apostle and martyr*

O F THE LITTLE THAT IS KNOWN about St. Peter's brother and fellow fisherman, perhaps the most interesting fact is that Andrew was the first disciple Jesus called. At the time Andrew was a follower of the prophet John the Baptist, but when he heard Jesus identified as the "Lamb of God," he was immediately curious to learn more. He spent the rest of the day in the company of the man whom he realized was the long-awaited Messiah.

A FISHERMAN'S SKILLS

Yet Andrew was an ordinary working man with no great accomplishments behind him or future in front of him. He was typical of the sort of person whom Jesus chose as his "fishers of men." Their qualities were the same as those that made them good fishermen: They needed patience, perseverance, and courage when the going was rough, and an eye for the right moment to cast their net. What Andrew lacked in social standing and intellect, he made up for with such human attributes as would turn him into an effective apostle for Christ.

He helped in the Feeding of the Five Thousand miracle by distributing the loaves and fishes, appropriate for a man of his trade; and he heard Jesus's prophecies about the end of time. Both Jesus and John the Baptist preached about the coming Last Judgment and the need to follow holy paths of righteousness. Andrew was one among many who joined ranks with itinerant prophets of the time.

LATER TRADITION

According to a fourth-century Jewish historian, Andrew was a missionary to Scythia, and it is possible that he preached in Russia, hence his patronage of that country. An even later tradition says he was martyred at Patras, in Greece, by being crucified on a diagonal (saltire) cross. According to legend, a figure by the name of St. Rule obeyed what he took to be divine instructions revealed in a dream and carried St. Andrew's relics from Patras to Fife in Scotland where they were buried. Consequently the fisherman became patron of the Scots. The medieval town that grew up around the shrine was renamed after him and became a pilgrimage site.

BANNER OF THE SCOTS

◆

According to tradition, King Hungus of the Picts, predecessors to the Scots, saw a transverse cross in the sky above his army on the battlefield. Their subsequent victory inspired him to adopt the saltire cross as a national symbol, and it has remained on the flag of Scotland ever since.

ABOVE *Ancient written tradition links St. Andrew with Greece. He became a key source of apostolic authority for the Eastern Church, centered at Constantinople, in opposition to Rome, which claimed the primacy of Sts. Peter and Paul.*

ABOVE *St. Luke writing his Gospel, with the symbol of his evangelism, the ox, in the foreground.*

LUKE (FIRST CENTURY)

FEAST DAY:	*October 18*
SYMBOLS IN ART:	*Calf*
PATRONAGE:	*Doctors, surgeons, artists*
PAINTINGS:	*Guernico,* St. Luke Displaying a Painting of the Virgin; *Hals, Frans,* St. Luke;
	Weyden, Rogier van der, St. Luke Drawing the Portrait of the Madonna
PROFILE:	*Greek physician, apostle, evangelist, and author of the Acts of the Apostles*

O F THE FOUR EVANGELISTS, Luke wrote most for the ordinary person. He directed his Gospel to the non-Jewish world, and in its sequel, Acts of the Apostles, he recorded the early spread of Christianity from Jerusalem, through the empire to Rome, center of the pagan world. His primary source for Acts was his companion St. Paul, who referred to Luke as "our dear friend, the doctor."

In choosing to arrange his material in this way Luke showed Christ's salvation to be open to all, not only or even primarily the Jews. To illustrate this point he introduced events and parables from sources not used by the first two evangelists, Matthew and Mark. Much-loved stories such as the parables of the Good Samaritan and the Prodigal Son are exclusive to Luke. Women figure more prominently in his narratives too; and in his account of the Passion one of the thieves that is crucified with Jesus goes to Heaven, showing how the Gospel addresses the outcasts and underprivileged in society.

ABOVE *A 17th-century unknown French artist's impression of the evangelist receiving divine inspiration.*

MEDICAL MAN

The compassion of Luke's literary works reflects something of the character of the man as well as his evangelical purpose. A medical doctor by profession, he would have witnessed much suffering in his working life. The knowledge and means of treatment at the time were limited. Medical schools in Roman Europe taught the rudiments of anatomy and medical care, and crude surgery could be performed, though without anesthetic and at considerable expense. Luke himself records how one woman with a hemorrhage had spent all her money on doctors and was no better! Her treatment probably would have included herbal remedies, which were more popular and affordable in Palestine.

EMBLEMS OF DEDICATION

Tradition holds that Luke was a painter as well, and that he produced at least one icon of the Virgin Mary. This explains his patronage of artists as well as of doctors and surgeons. It is thought that his evangelistic work is represented by the calf or ox on account of the sacrifice of such an animal in the temple described at the opening of his Gospel. The sacrificial animal was regarded as a suitable symbol for one whose life and work were conducted for the welfare of others.

JOSEPH OF ARIMATHEA (FIRST CENTURY)

FEAST DAY: *March 17*
SYMBOLS IN ART: *Shroud, crown of thorns, nails, altar cruets*
PATRONAGE: *Funeral directors, undertakers, tin miners*
PAINTINGS: *Fra Angelico,* The Deposition*; Gerard David,* The Deposition
PROFILE: *Member of the Jewish council in Jerusalem and secret follower of Christ*

MORE LEGEND THAN FACT has fastened to this mysterious, noble figure whose unexpected devotion to Christ after his death has given rise to much speculation about Joseph's life.

THE LORD'S UNDERTAKER

After Jesus had died Joseph obtained permission from Pilate to take the body down from the cross. With the help of Nicodemus, another secret disciple, he wrapped it in a linen cloth and carried it to a new tomb, which Joseph may have bought for his own burial.

He was clearly a man of means. As well as giving up a portion of his tomb, which would have been costly to have cut from the rock, he prepared the body for burial with expensive ointments normally reserved for royalty. It is thought that Joseph, a member of the aristocracy, may have been related to Jesus and that his lavish embalming of the body was performed in recognition of the Messiah's royal lineage. If Jesus was a rightful pretender to the Jewish throne, his epitaph "King of the Jews" would make more sense.

LEGEND OF THE HOLY GRAIL

The legend of the Holy Grail relates that Joseph collected drops of Jesus's blood in the chalice used for the Last Supper, and that in 63 B.C.E. he carried it via Gaul to Glastonbury in England. The cup was buried under a thorn tree that is said to have sprouted from Joseph's walking stick. According to tradition, the tree blossomed only at Christmas, but in Oliver Cromwell's day it was considered to be idolatrous and was cut down. Nevertheless, cuttings from the tree, *Crataegus oxyacantha*, still flourish in the neighborhood and blossom at that festive time. In Joseph's honor a thatched church was built in Glastonbury and his body was reputedly buried there.

TIN MERCHANT

There is a legend that Joseph visited England on business as a tin merchant, knowing of the extensive resources of this metal in Cornwall, in the southwest of the country. The tradition that he was accompanied by the young Jesus on this expedition provided the inspiration for William Blake's famous hymn "Jerusalem."

ABOVE *A 15th-century French manuscript illumination
focuses on the diminutive figure of Joseph of Arimathea
collecting the Savior's blood in the Holy Grail.*

CECILIA (THIRD CENTURY)

FEAST DAY: *November 22*
SYMBOLS IN ART: *Organ or lute*
PATRONAGE: *Musicians, composers, singers, and makers of musical instruments*
PAINTINGS: *Artemisia Gentileschi*, St. Cecilia Playing the Lute
PROFILE: *Roman aristocrat and martyr*

ABOVE *A popularized interpretation of St. Cecilia in post-revolutionary, 19th-century France.*

AN HEIRESS OF ROME became a *cause célèbre* in Christian circles when she stuck obstinately to her beliefs and challenged the ancient custom of arranged marriage. Although she deferred to her father's wishes by going ahead with the bond to a fellow noble, she confirmed her vows to God on her wedding day and remained determined to maintain her viginity. Her fortitude and conviction of belief so impressed her bridegroom that he converted to the faith too and respected her maidenhood.

That Cecilia dedicated herself to God was symbolized in the wedding ceremony. While musicians played out her nuptials, she is said to have sung in her heart to Heaven, a pledge of faith that turned Cecilia into the patroness of musicians.

It is possible that Cecilia's biographical records were misinterpreted, resulting in her being credited with playing the organ herself. According to tradition she combined instrumental with vocal music, and when the Academy of Music was founded in Rome in the sixteenth century she was made its patroness. From there she became patron saint of church music in general, and is now invoked by Cecilian musical societies for her guidance.

IN PRAISE OF MUSIC

The primary purpose of religious music was to lift hearts toward God. By joining the heavenly spirits in songs of praise and adoration, choristers induced themselves to holy jubilation. St. John Chrysostom extolled the good effects of sacred music, asserting that devout psalmody kindled the fire of divine love in the soul. On the other hand, it was also said that too much time spent being idly amused in music bewitches the senses and dissipates the mind. Soft and sentimental melodies should always be avoided, since they poison virtue and corrupt the heart!

Cecilia's devotion was legendary. Although she was brought up a Christian, the attitudes of Roman society often conflicted with her faith. Beneath the fine robes befitting her rank, she wore a coarse garment in self-mortification. She fasted for several days a week and in other respects was an exemplar of a faith still the object of persecution in the empire. Both Cecilia's husband and his brother fell foul of the authorities for their creed, and eventually Cecilia herself paid with her life, though not by her first punishment. A sentence of death by suffocation in her bathroom failed despite the fact that the furnace was fed with seven times its normal amount of fuel. Beheading was more effective.

See also DUNSTAN *page 144*

MARTIN OF TOURS (C. 316–397)

FEAST DAY:	*November 11*
SYMBOLS IN ART:	*Cloak, donkey, globe of fire, goose*
PATRONAGE:	*Horsemen, soldiers, drapers, tailors, France*
PAINTINGS:	*Brueghel, Jan the Elder,* St. Martin; *El Greco,* St. Martin and the Beggar; *Martini, Simone,* The Dream of St. Martin
PROFILE:	*Bishop, father of French monasticism, and conscientious objector*

ABOVE *St. Martin of Tours.*

T HIS HOLY MAN of the Dark Ages was one of the first non-martyrs to be publicly venerated as a saint. He started out as a reluctant soldier in the Roman army guarding the frontier against barbarian invasion. As a cavalry officer at Amiens, in modern France, Martin was so moved by the plight of a shivering beggar that he tore his cloak in two and gave one half to him. It proved to be a seminal moment as that night he saw a vision of Christ in the man, and converted as a result. In truth, the experience confirmed his Christian inclinations. Having formally adopted a pacifist faith, he no longer felt able to continue in armed combat. His request to be released from the army in about 340 was met with the taunt of cowardice, to which he retorted that he would stand on the battlefield between the two opposing lines as a demonstration of his conscientious objection. He was duly granted a discharge, and lived for a while as a recluse on an island off the Ligurian coast of Italy.

ABOVE *Whether chivalrous knight or muleteer, St. Martin was regarded as a model of active Christian virtue.*

PIONEER IN RURAL FRANCE

At Ligugé, he founded the first monastery in Gaul. As bishop of Tours from 372, Martin made it his mission to extend Christianity in Gaul beyond the urban centers, to which the Church was more or less confined at the time. He ventured forth into remote places where pagan superstition and sorcery governed the minds of rural peasants. His warmth and love won over many to the faith, and miracles were attributed to him, such as cures for leprosy and even raising one man from the dead.

PATRON OF HORSEMEN

His immense popularity in the Middle Ages turned Martin into the patron of medieval knights and horsemen. Many churches across Europe were dedicated to him, including, most famously, St. Martin-in-the-Fields in London. Horseshoes were sometimes nailed to the doors of his churches as a votive offering showing a commitment to his cause.

See also GEORGE *page 94*

JEROME (347–419)

FEAST DAY:	*September 30*
SYMBOLS IN ART:	*Lion*
PATRONAGE:	*Librarians*
PAINTINGS:	*Bosch, Hieronymus, St. Jerome in Prayer; Caravaggio, St. Jerome; El Greco, St. Jerome; Titian, St. Jerome*
PROFILE:	*One of the four great Doctors of the Western Church*

BIOGRAPHIES OF SAINTS often reveal a crucial life-changing moment, perhaps the result of an inner crisis. In Jerome's case, all lay beyond his control. His fortunes changed so radically that he must have felt like a man falling from grace.

Despite a Christian upbringing in metropolitan Rome, Jerome felt a calling to the ascetic life of the desert. At the age of 27 he went to live with hermits in Syria, where he learned Hebrew and became a priest. His biblical scholarship and knowledge of classical languages came to the attention of Pope Damasus, who was anxious to solve the growing problem in the fourth-century Western Church of not having a good Latin Bible for use in Mass. Existing versions were poor, with awkward translations of the original Greek and numerous transcription errors. So Damasus appointed Jerome as his private secretary with a charge to produce an authoritative Latin version of the Gospels.

The refined scholar moved back to Rome where his disdain for its worldly life did not prevent him from becoming immensely popular. In one of his many letters, he writes, "All Rome resounded with my praises ... Men called me holy, men called me humble and eloquent."* In fact he was so popular that he was put forward as a candidate to succeed Damasus.

ILL WIND OF CHANGE

On failing to secure election to the papal chair, however, Jerome found to his dismay that he had fallen out of favor. His intemperate spirit made him enemies. The letter he wrote aboard the ship that was to carry him from Italy forever is full of the invective for which he became notorious: "I am said to be a slippery knave, one who lies and deceives others by Satanic art ... some kissed my hands, yet attacked me with the tongues of vipers; sympathy was on their lips, but malignant joy in their hearts ... such is the company in which I have lived for almost three years."*

RETREAT IN THE HOLY LAND

Jerome settled in Bethlehem in 386, accompanied by members of his ascetic group. One of them was St. Paula, whose fortune paid for the building of monasteries, a hospice, and a free school at which Jerome taught local children. He spent the next 20 years on his greatest work, the translation of the Bible from the original Hebrew and Greek into Latin, which became known as the "Vulgate."

The loving side of Jerome's nature was allowed to flower in Bethlehem. As spiritual guide to nuns and monks, he frequently gave shelter to refugees from Rome after the Goths invaded the city in 410.

LOVER OF ARGUMENT

It was part of Jerome's complex character that behind his kindly nature was a punctilious scholar who could be roused to fury with tongue and pen alike. He was frequently embroiled in the theological disputes of his day—on celibacy, original sin, and divine grace—and stopped at nothing to expose error. He called his erstwhile friend Rufinus a "scorpion," and he dismissed the British theologian Pelagius as "one whose wits have been dulled by too much Scottish porridge."

Yet he knew how to praise: "Of all the ladies of Rome but one had the power to subdue me. The psalms were her only songs, the Gospel her whole speech, continence her one indulgence, fasting the staple of her life." The woman in question was St. Paula of Rome.

---

*J. Stevenson (ed.), *Creeds, Councils, and Controversies*   *See also* AUGUSTINE *page 140*

ABOVE *Sitting amid a scaffolded ruin, Jerome contemplates the life of Christ after his own rejection by the people of Rome.*

ABOVE *The gifted Latin scholar St. Augustine of Hippo (left) became the most influential Christian theologian after St. Paul. His reassuring words about God's ever-flowing grace helped to dispel fears of damnation that overshadowed medieval cloisters.*

AUGUSTINE (354–430)

FEAST DAY:	*August 28*
SYMBOLS IN ART:	*Child, dove, pen, shell*
PATRONAGE:	*Brewers, theologians*
PAINTINGS:	*Coello, Claudio,* The Triumph of St. Augustine;
	El Greco, St. Augustine of Hippo
PROFILE:	*North African bishop and Doctor of the Church; author*
	of Confessions *and* The City of God

THE MOST INFLUENTIAL THEOLOGIAN of early Christendom was no saint in his youth. He was born to a pagan father and Christian mother, and his life was marked by inner conflicts. His mother, Monica, despaired at his dissolute ways as a youth, especially his "living in sin" with a common-law wife for 14 years. He himself grew increasingly anxious about his spiritual life but could not commit to God in his heart, famously praying, "please make me chaste—but not just yet."

ABOVE *A 14th-century study of the fierce upholder of orthodoxy.*

CONVERSION EXPERIENCE

Disgusted by the barbarity of the Old Testament, he joined the Manichees, a heterodox Christian group that believed the God of the Old Testament to be evil and in constant cosmic battle with the good God of Christ. In Milan he came under the influence of Ambrose, who set his mind more at ease, teaching him that the Old Testament stories were allegories, not to be taken literally. But still Augustine yearned for spiritual fulfillment.

Then one day it happened. As he describes in his *Confessions*, he was sitting in the garden listening to local children singing a song that repeated the line "read it, read it." Taking this to be a call from God, he opened the Bible at random, determined to follow whatever it might say. He found himself reading a passage from Paul's Letter to the Romans, Chapter 13, Verses 12–14, telling the reader to put aside his carnal desires and don the armor of Christ. Augustine sighed with relief. "It was as though the light of faith flooded into my heart and all the darkness of doubt was dispelled," he said.

CHAMPION OF THE TRUE CHURCH

Augustine was baptized and before long the people of Hippo in Numidia, modern-day Algeria, clamored for him to be made their bishop. As such, he fought heresy on all fronts. He challenged his former colleagues, the Manichees, by teaching that God's Creation was all good and that evil was merely the absence of good in the world. He preached that the Church was a mixed field of wheat and weeds, of believers and nonbelievers, growing together until the harvest.

His most famous contribution to orthodox doctrine was his definition of original sin as the inherited guilt of the first man, Adam, and that human beings could only obey God through his grace. Augustine's teachings were used by later reformers, especially John Calvin, who stressed the idea that people were predestined to either Heaven or Hell.

THE CITY OF GOD

Augustine's best-known work was written in response to the fall of Rome in 410. Some Romans blamed the calamity on the abandonment of the pagan gods. In the pessimistic tone characteristic of his later life, Augustine responded by describing two cities, one created by worldly love, the other by heavenly love. Amid the disintegrating Roman Empire and Vandal invaders at the gates of his own town of Hippo, he taught Christians simply to endure the tribulations of the world and seek the peace of the heavenly city.

See also MONICA *page 15,* AMBROSE *page 18*

DAVID (DIED 601)

FEAST DAY: *March 1*
SYMBOLS IN ART: *Dove*
PATRONAGE: *Wales, poets*
PAINTINGS: *None known*
PROFILE: *Abbot-bishop, by tradition related to King Arthur; known as Dewi in Welsh*

ABOVE *A stained glass representation of St. David, patron of bards and poets.*

THE ONLY WELSHMAN to be canonized in the Western Church has an unreliable history but one with sufficient evidence to suggest he was the most important British churchman of the early Dark Ages. In the period between the departure of the Romans from British shores and the invasion of Saxons and Angles from the continent, it was probably the Christianity of St. David, Celtic son of King Sant of South Wales, who spread the faith early in western Britain.

He founded ten monasteries and became bishop and abbot of one of them at Menevia, the former Roman port in Pembrokeshire, in West Wales, now called St. David's after him. This port was the usual embarkation point for Ireland, and it is thought that early seafaring missionaries to the country may have been instructed by David. His main theological achievement came at the Synod of Brevi, at which he successfully fought the Pelagian heresy over divine grace.

DILIGENT AND SOBER

Nicknamed the "waterman," possibly on account of his abstinence from drinking beer or wine, David became a paragon of monastic virtue. His monks were taught to follow a harsh regime based on the early Egyptian model practiced by St. Antony in the desert. Heavy manual labor was the order of the day, without the usual aid of cattle to till the ground. They would study the scriptures in silence and never speak in the monastery unless it was necessary. A meager vegetarian diet, with bread and water, sustained them through long hours of devotion to their tasks. David's favorite exercises were genuflections and total immersion in cold water.

LEGENDS OF AVALON

According to medieval historians, including the notoriously unreliable Geoffrey of Monmouth, David was related to King Arthur, either as his nephew or uncle. One of David's ten monasteries was reputedly built at Glastonbury (Avalon), traditional burial site of the warrior king. He is also credited with adding a chancel to the thatched church erected for Joseph of Arimathea, whose legend of the Holy Grail is associated with the site. The relics of St. David were said to have been transported to Glastonbury in the tenth century before being instated in the present cathedral of his home town.

On St. David's Day, Welshmen used to wear a leek in their hats, supposedly in memory of an occasion when the vegetable was donned to distinguish themselves from English troops on the battlefield.

See also ANTONY *page 30,* JOSEPH OF ARIMATHEA *page 134*

ISIDORE OF SEVILLE (560–636)

FEAST DAY:	*April 4*
SYMBOLS IN ART:	*Bees, pen, book*
PATRONAGE:	*School children; proposed for computer technicians and users of the Internet*
PAINTINGS:	*None known*
PROFILE:	*Archbishop of Seville, educator, and Doctor of the Church*

WITH GREGORY THE GREAT, Isidore shares the unofficial title of "Schoolmaster of the Middle Ages." He turned his extensive studies in religion, history, geography, astronomy, and science into an encyclopedia of knowledge of the time. It was the first to be compiled and it remained a valuable source of reference throughout the Middle Ages. His breadth of knowledge was so great that he led the field of candidates to be patron of computer users and the Internet in 1999.

TOUGH BEGINNINGS

Prolific though his works were—including a dictionary, a history of the Goths, and a history of the world from the time of Creation—Isidore was a poor student according to his elder brother and educator. He was frequently punished for being slow. In fact his brother's treatment was so harsh that Isidore ran away. His later accomplishments show him to be both intelligent and diligent, but first he had to overcome his feelings of failure and rejection.

THE DRIP, DRIP OF LEARNING

One day he noticed water dripping onto a rock as he sat nearby. Although the drops were small and carried no force, he could see that over time they had worn a hole in the rock. This made him realize that, if he continued to study, his little progress would eventually turn into a great body of work. With new confidence he returned to his brother and, although he was immediately shut away in a cell, he set to work with fresh determination. Despite this severity, Isidore became the most learned man of his age and an enthusiastic educator.

ABOVE *The early Christian compiler of knowledge, St. Isidore of Seville, is today invoked by Internet users searching for information.*

SCHOOLS FOR EVERYONE

Upon the death of his brother, Isidore succeeded him as archbishop of Seville and for the next 37 years he tirelessly campaigned to improve education in Spain. On account of his exceptional merit as a teacher, Isidore commanded great authority in the Spanish church councils of the seventh century. His notable achievement was the decree that every diocese in the country should have a cathedral school. Not only would many more children be given the opportunity for an education, but he broadened the range of studies beyond the narrow classical curriculum to include such areas of study as the arts, medicine, and law.

See also JOHN BOSCO *page 152*

DUNSTAN (C. 910–988)

FEAST DAY:	*May 19*
SYMBOLS IN ART:	*Tongs, dove, harp*
PATRONAGE:	*Armorers, blacksmiths, goldsmiths, jewelers, lighthouse keepers, locksmiths, musicians, singers*
PAINTINGS:	*None known*
PROFILE:	*Archbishop of Canterbury who established the Rule of St. Benedict in England*

St. Dunstan and the Debil.

ABOVE *A legend circulated in medieval times that St. Dunstan, patron of blacksmiths, seized the devil by the nose with a pair of pincers and would not release him until he promised to tempt the archbishop no longer.*

IT HAS BEEN SAID that English history found its shape in the tenth century and that St. Dunstan was responsible for it. He came to the fore when the monastic life of the country lay virtually extinct after the ravages of Danish raids. Almost single-handedly he restored that lone beacon of civilization and, at the same time, so reformed its character that medieval England would be changed forever.

Dunstan was able to take advantage of weak and short-lived kingships characteristic of his time. Born into a noble Anglo-Saxon family, he was from an early age walking among the ruling classes of Wessex (kingdom of the west Saxons), and at the age of 18 was made Abbot of Glastonbury.

CIVILIZER OF ENGLAND

The restoration process began, and in so doing Dunstan turned Glastonbury into a great center of civilization. He himself was an accomplished scholar and artist. He painted and illuminated manuscripts; created beautiful designs in embroidery; and worked metal, making bells and sacred vessels to replace those lost to the looters. The beauty of his harp playing and singing, like all his artistic works, inspired others to learn the various skills of craftsmanship in what became an infectious spirit of aesthetic enterprise.

MONASTIC REFORMER

Dunstan's talents were clearly many and he became a sought-after man in the political sphere too. However, his uncompromising views on morality did not always sit well with the nobles: They took umbrage at being chastised for lewd behavior. His advice to make peace with the Danes had its critics, too, and he soon found himself exiled in Flanders. It was here, though, that he discovered the perfect example of the monastic life in the Benedictine style. He determined to establish this rule in his homeland.

On a summons to return from the new king, Edgar, Dunstan saw his fortunes rise fast. He was made royal chief adviser, and in quick succession was appointed Bishop of Worcester and London, and finally Archbishop of Canterbury in 961.

With papal authority, he set about his reforms. In conference with all of England's bishops, abbots, and abbesses, he drew up a national code of monastic observance based on the more humane and flexible style of the Benedictine Rule. Furthermore, he placed the monasteries in the service of the public, who could now benefit from their expertise in fields such as medicine, agriculture, horticulture, and even hospitality.

See also CECILIA *page 136*

Isidore the Farm Laborer (C. 1080–1130)

FEAST DAY:	*May 15*
SYMBOLS IN ART:	*Sickle*
PATRONAGE:	*Farmers, agricultural workers, laborers, ranchers, rural communities, livestock, child death, Madrid*
PAINTINGS:	*None known*
PROFILE:	*Spanish plowman with exemplary piety*

F EW MEN OF SUCH HUMBLE OCCUPATION as Isidore's are canonized. The loyal farmhand to a Spanish landowner near Madrid achieved sanctity in his lifetime by striving to do nothing more ambitious than serve God with complete devotion throughout his ordinary life.

Yet it took the personal tragedy of losing his only child to set him on this course of dedication. He and his wife saw their son's death as a sign that God intended them to be childless. Thereafter, they obeyed a vow of celibacy and led lives utterly committed to serving God.

THE HOLY PLOWMAN

Isidore would rise early enough to go to church each day before work. Frequently he would arrive late, to the consternation of his master and fellow laborers, who said they had to carry his burden. His reply was that service to his main master must come first. The repetitious nature of plowing the fields had its own rhythm enabling him to spend long periods in prayer.

When Isidore died, his reputation for holiness grew even more. People prayed for his intercession and miraculous cures were reported during the late medieval period. By the seventeenth century, Spanish kings and queens were enlisting his aid in matters of health and war, even though he was yet to be officially declared a saint.

MIRACLES AND LEGENDS ATTRIBUTED TO ISIDORE

- After arriving late for work because of time spent at Mass, Isidore was seen in the field accompanied by angels leading a second team of white oxen plowing the earth.

- After he had given away half his load of corn to hungry birds in winter, the remaining half produced twice the amount of flour.

- In a vision, Isidore is said to have guided King Alphonsus of Castile to a place where he could successfully make a surprise attack on his enemy, the Moors.

- In 1615 the humble servant's relics were moved into Philip III's bedroom, whereupon the king immediately recovered from a serious fever. After this, the king petitioned the pope to have the man canonized, which he was in 1622.

BELOW *Attired in 18th-century Castilian dress, the humble laborer is presented as an inspiration to all who work on farms in Spain.*

ALBERT THE GREAT (1200–1280)

FEAST DAY:	*November 15*
SYMBOLS IN ART:	*Books, pulpit, palm*
PATRONAGE:	*Medical technicians, scientists*
PAINTINGS:	*da Modena, Tommaso, Albertus Magnus (fresco)*
PROFILE:	*German Dominican friar, bishop, philosopher, and theologian; made Doctor of the Church in 1931*

ABOVE *Born in Swabia, in southern Germany, the "Universal Doctor" moved to several cities of Europe, including Padua, Cologne, and Paris.*

THE ONLY SCHOLAR of his age to be called "the Great" helped to lay the foundations of modern science. His experiments and classification of the natural sciences ran to 38 volumes, and covered such diverse subjects as chemistry, geography, astronomy, and physiology. He was also the first man in the West to expand on the teachings of the ancient Greek philosopher Aristotle, whose ideas remained hidden during the Dark Ages. In the midst of these studies, the question in his mind of how faith should be related to reason constantly presented itself.

COMPATIBLE FAITH AND SCIENCE

As more and more about the world was understood through the use of reasoning, so less seemed to be explained by the providence of faith. Debate raged about whether the knowledge of Creation as supposedly revealed by God was compromised by that acquired through man's own intelligence. For Albert, there was no contradiction between the two routes to knowledge. There was no "double truth," as some asserted: One for faith and another for reason. All that is really true, he said, was joined in harmony, though some mysteries can be grasped only by faith alone. One of the Church's best minds on the matter was Albert's illustrious pupil, Thomas Aquinas.

ROCKETS, ROBOTS, AND EVOLUTION

Albert was no bookish scholar by nature, preferring to conduct his research in the field and through experimentation. He was forever asking questions of fishermen, hunters, bird catchers, and beekeepers, taking down copious notes. He traveled through nearly all of Europe in his exhaustive quest.

Scientific experiments were his forte, and some of his investigations established the groundwork for subsequent developments. At a time when conventional thinking held the world to be flat, he demonstrated that it was round; his views, it is said, led to the later discovery of America. He described devices with which to power rockets, and in so doing contributed to the founding of firearms in the following century. With the British scientist Roger Bacon, he was even among the first to construct robots, designing a moving iron man.

Albert never regarded any of these clever inventions as obstructive to the faith—after all, rocketry could be put to good use in defending Christendom against the infidel Saracens in the next Crusade, which Albert supported. However, there was one area of investigation that probably caused him some concern. In his classification of the animal world, he must have had an inkling of man's relationship to primates. In categorizing man alongside "apes" and "animals," Albert contributed to the theory of evolution which tormented the Church in the nineteenth century.

See also THOMAS AQUINAS *page 24*

Albertus Magnus.

ABOVE *On canonizing Albert in 1931, Pope Pius XI said that the Dominican friar possessed a "rare and divine gift: Scientific instinct," which he hoped would be an inspiration to the modern age.*

ABOVE *St. Francis of Sales lived by his maxim that "the measure of love is to love without measure."*

FRANCIS OF SALES (1567–1622)

FEAST DAY:	*January 24*
SYMBOLS IN ART:	*None*
PATRONAGE:	*Journalists and writers*
PAINTINGS:	*Tiepolo, Giambattista*, St. Francis of Sales
PROFILE:	*Bishop of Geneva, Doctor of the Church, founder of the Order of the Visitation (1610), and devotional writer*

ONE OF THE MOST IMPORTANT FIGURES of the Roman Catholic Counter-Reformation brought the devotional life out of the cloister and into the daily lives of ordinary men and women. Perfection is possible for everyone, he maintained, not only for the professionally religious.

Born into an aristocratic family of Savoy, Francis made it his first task to convince his father that the priesthood, not the law in which he trained, was his vocation. With many areas of the Church now dominated by Protestantism, the Roman Catholic Church was in great need of missionary effort. As an ordained priest, Francis was sent to Geneva to help win back those who had joined the Calvinists in Chablais on the south shore of Lake Geneva. Tirelessly, his coterie of missionaries traveled the region, undeterred by the insults and occasional beatings they received; attempts were even made on Francis's life.

POWER OF THE PEN

Despite the setbacks, Francis persevered, constantly seeking new ways to reach the hearts and minds of the people. One way was to write leaflets, which he distributed widely. The simple, loving piety of these brief tracts persuaded lapsed Catholics of the truth of their original faith, and by the end of his mission he is said to have converted some 8,000 people. Even a Calvinist minister of Geneva remarked, "If we honored any man as a saint, I know no one since the days of the apostles more worthy of it than this man."[*]

EVERYMAN'S DEVOTION

Francis became famous for his writing. Although many classics of spirituality down the ages had inspired monks and nuns, none reached out to the ordinary person who felt too worldly and busy to try to emulate such holiness as described in these works. But it was not so hard to achieve, according to Francis of Sales. In his *Introduction to the Devout Life* (1609) he says devotion is easy, or at least much easier than most would expect. With charm and a psychologist's skill, he offers spiritual guidance for the common man. A busy person can practice the contemplative life anywhere—on the street, at work, or among the family. Everyone is capable of silent mental prayer, he says, and the daily round of tasks always presents opportunities for acts of self-sacrifice to those who would seize them.

Another renowned work of St. Francis of Sales is *Treatise on the Love of God* (1616).

[*]A. Hamon, *Life of St. Francis de Sales*

See also JOHN BOSCO *page 152*

LOUISE DE MARILLAC (1591–1660)

FEAST DAY:	*March 15*
SYMBOLS IN ART:	*Breton dress*
PATRONAGE:	*Social workers, widows*
PAINTINGS:	*None known*
PROFILE:	*Co-founder with St. Vincent de Paul of the Daughters of Charity*

ABOVE *St. Louise de Marillac, a matron nurse whose compassion matched her endurance.*

HAVING LOST BOTH PARENTS by the age of 15 and nursed her husband through a fatal illness, Louise wished to devote the rest of her life to the service of God. She met Vincent de Paul, who at this time was setting up a charity by which wealthy women in Paris would help the sick and poor of the city.

FIRST WOMEN SOCIAL WORKERS

The group was radical in its day for not being a religious order. Its members were not nuns shut away from the deprivations of society, but Christian women ministering daily to its victims. As Vincent de Paul said, "Your convent will be the house of the sick, your cell a hired room, your cloister the city streets or the hospital wards."

However, many of the aristocratic women who had offered themselves to this task found that, despite admirable intentions, they were unable to cope with the appalling conditions. Nursing the poor in their own homes, caring for neglected children, and sometimes having to handle aggressive menfolk demanded a thick skin as well as Christian charity. De Paul recognized in Louise the qualities of endurance, courage, and intelligence required of someone who could partner him in this noble undertaking. As well as nursing the sick herself, she would train working-class women in the task, an activity conducted from her own home in Paris, which she gave over to the cause.

DAUGHTERS OF CHARITY

These dedicated activities proved to be the foundation of a worldwide operation known as the Daughters of Charity, which in turn spawned numerous Roman Catholic congregations of noncloistered women who called themselves the Sisters of Charity. They offered their services in various capacities of social work, but in particular nursing, which in wartime earned them the title of "Angels of the Battlefield."

By the time of Louise's death, the sick and poor were looked after in 26 parishes in Paris. In France as a whole more than 40 houses of the Sisters had been established. By the end of the twentieth century, the Daughters of Charity made up the largest single congregation of religious women. The traditional garb of peasant women from Breton was adopted to form the Sisters' distinctive habit of a gray tunic with white headdress.

See also VINCENT DE PAUL *page 61*

JOHN-BAPTIST DE LA SALLE (1651–1719)

FEAST DAY:	*April 7*
SYMBOLS IN ART:	*None*
PATRONAGE:	*Schoolteachers*
PAINTINGS:	*None known*
PROFILE:	*French priest, educator, and founder of the Brothers of the Christian School*

THE MAN WHO WAS DECLARED patron of all schoolteachers gave up a life of wealth, noble ease, and ultimately his priestly duties to pioneer new schooling for the working classes. A chance encounter with a stranger in his home town of Rheims sparked his interest in the education of the poor and he supported the man's ambition to set up two schools. Their ideas, however, were naïve and the enterprise ran into problems with the fellow teachers whom they hired. However, John-Baptist de La Salle kept faith with his convictions and soon his experiment was working.

THE NOVEL IDEA OF CLASS TEACHING

Until this time, academic instruction was given on an individual basis, in Latin. John-Baptist introduced to Western society the idea of delivering lessons in the vernacular language, in this case, French, to a class of pupils, who were bound by a rule of silence. To provide religious instruction, he introduced the idea of Sunday School, which also gave technical education for aspiring artisans.

Not everyone, though, approved of his innovations. Professional schoolmasters dismissed his novelty as a fad. Traditionalists thought the working classes should be taught only manual skills. Others praised his initiative, which he funded entirely from the proceeds of his own inheritance. He opened four schools and named his community the Brothers of the Christian Schools. To maintain equality and an ethos dedicated strictly to teaching, it was agreed that all members should be laymen. Accordingly, John-Baptist gave up his priestly role and income.

FIRST TEACHER-TRAINING COLLEGES

Soon, parish priests sent him young men to be trained as schoolmasters, who then returned to teach his method in local schools. In this way his educational revolution spread through the region of Champagne. Demand was such that in 1687 he set up a full-time teacher-training college in Rheims, the first of its kind, which was followed by others in Paris and Saint-Denis.

Other notable achievements include his educating, at the invitation of the exiled King James II of England, of 50 sons of the gentry in his royal entourage. John-Baptist also created a reform school for juvenile delinquents.

ABOVE *St. John-Baptist gave up the priesthood to concentrate on teaching.*

* M. Walsh, *Butler's Lives of the Saints.*

JOHN BOSCO (1815–1888)

FEAST DAY:	*January 31*
SYMBOLS IN ART:	*None*
PATRONAGE:	*Apprentices, boys, school children*
PAINTINGS:	*None known*
PROFILE:	*Italian educator and founder of the Salesian Order; also called Don Bosco*

AS A POOR BOY OF TURIN, this future saint had a dream when he was nine, showing him his vocation. Surrounded by a crowd of violent screaming children, John tried to pacify them, at first by reasoning, then by resorting to force. Suddenly a mysterious woman appeared and said to him, "Softly, softly … if you wish to win them. Take your shepherd's staff and lead them to pasture."* As she spoke, the children were transformed into wild beasts, then into lambs. From that moment, John realized that his duty was to help poor boys.

Raised in poverty himself, after his father had died while he was young, John had to wear second-hand clothes in order to begin his training as a priest. It was at theological college in Turin that he first pursued his calling by devoting his Sundays to gathering waifs and homeless apprentices from the slums, and running a sort of Sunday School and recreation center.

WORKSHOPS AND NIGHT SCHOOL

John developed this work further with the help of his mother, who acted as his housekeeper in the rooms they rented next to the oratory where he was training. He started taking in destitute children and, before long, was giving shelter to about 40 boys, most of them poor apprentices who worked by day in the city. They attended his chapel and evening classes, but John soon found that any good he was doing was negated by influences from the streets.

He resolved to set up apprenticeships himself at home. As well as running a night school, he opened two workshops to train tailors and shoemakers in 1853. It was so successful that the following year he founded a congregation for the purpose, which he called the Salesians, after St. Francis of Sales, whom he so admired. Within 2 years there were 150 resident boys, 4 workshops, and a printing press. The scope of training broadened to include many different trades, such as farming and metalwork. When the founder died, by which time the society had received the pope's blessing, well over 700 Salesians operated worldwide.

With the help of a peasant woman, St. Mary Mazzarello, John founded a similar institution for girls, which he called the Daughters of Mary, Help of Christians, which also found rapid success.

John Bosco was an enlightened innovator. He said he had no special system of education, but that his methods were aimed at preventing wrongdoing. He sought to make appealing whatever he presented, whether school subjects or religious practice. He is also credited with some miraculous events, which are well attested, such as the multiplication of food.

* M. Walsh, *Butler's Lives of the Saints.*

See also FRANCIS OF SALES *page 148*

ABOVE *A tile mosaic in Seville, Spain, is dedicated to St. John Bosco, who learned in the slums that preventing a wrong was the beginning of good.*

TERESA OF LISIEUX (1873–1897)

FEAST DAY:	*October 1*
SYMBOLS IN ART:	*Bunch of roses*
PATRONAGE:	*Florists and flower growers, foreign missions, sick people, AIDS sufferers, France, Russia*
PAINTINGS:	*None known*
PROFILE:	*French Carmelite nun; made a Doctor of the Church by John Paul II in 1997; also known as Teresa of the Little Jesus and the Little Flower*

OUTWARDLY ONE OF THE LEAST REMARKABLE of people was called the greatest saint of modern times by Pope Pius X, himself a saint. This he said prophetically before Teresa had even been beatified. Her spiritual autobiography, *The Story of a Soul*, in which she describes the "little way" of simplicity and daily duty, has become an inspiration to the ordinary faithful.

PATH OF TRUE HOLINESS

After her mother died when Teresa Martin was four, she followed two of her three sisters into the Carmelite convent at Lisieux, the town where her father had moved his family in order to be closer to their aunt. Teresa typified the inward-looking character of middle-class French Catholics of the nineteenth century. In her simple devotion to her religious duties, she reminded the world of the basic principles of a life dedicated to Christ—one of pure self-sacrifice, uncloaked by the strivings of the will, which may disguise itself in good public works. In Teresa the way of self-denial reached a level of serenity that required no supportive acts of mortification, practices that she dismissed as artificial aids obstructing the path to true holiness.

SHOWER OF ROSES

The fact that Teresa's cloistered life, beginning at age 15, was unremarkable was in part due to her discovery, at age 20, that she had tuberculosis. On her deathbed four years later, she said, "I do not intend to remain idle in heaven. My longing is to labor even there for the Church and souls."

Depictions of her holding a bunch of roses indicate her promise to "let fall from heaven a shower of roses." These floral symbols are thought to refer to miracles and other graces that those who seek her help through prayer will experience. Since her death, many people have testified to hearing her voice in their prayers. She was beloved of French troops in the trenches of World War I, and she was reported to have appeared several times to men during World War II, giving encouragement and even miraculous help to the Allied forces.

Several inspirational quotations are attributed to Teresa, among them these memorable ones*:

● "For me, prayer is a surge of the heart; it is a simple look turned toward heaven, it is a cry of recognition and of love, embracing both trial and joy."

● "Just as the sun shines simultaneously on the tall cedars and on each little flower as though it were alone on earth, so Our Lord is occupied particularly with each soul as though there were no others like it."

● *"Like the daisy
With the rosy calyx,
Me, tiny little flower
I open up to the sun."*

*From *Story of a Soul*.

<small>ABOVE</small> *St. Teresa of Lisieux in Normandy has such a large following that in 1997 her coffin began an eight-year world tour to commemorate the 100th anniversary of her death.*

JANUARY

1 Fulgentius; Joseph Tommasi; Odilo
2 **Basil the Great** (*see page 46*); Gregory of Nazianzus
3 **Geneviève** (*see page 97*)
4 Elizabeth Seton
5 John Nepomucene Neumann; **Simeon the Stylite** (West) (*see page 49*)
6 Peter of Canterbury
7 Canute Lavard; Lucian of Antioch
8 Gudula; Lucian of Beauvais; Pega; Severinus of Noricum
9 Adrian of Canterbury; Philip of Moscow
10 Peter Orseolo
11 Paulinus of Aquileia; Theodosius the Cenobiarch
12 Benedict (or Benet) Biscop; Tatiana
13 Antony Pucci; Hilary of Poitiers
14 Macrina the Elder
15 Ita; Macarius the Elder; Paul the Hermit
16 Berard and his companions; Fursey; Honoratus of Arles
17 **Antony of Egypt** (*see page 30*); Sulpicius
18 Margaret of Hungary; Prisca
19 Canute IV; Henry of Uppsala; Wulfstan
20 Euthymius the Great; Fabian; **Sebastian** (*see page 114*)
21 Agnes; Meinrad
22 Anastasius the Persian; Vincent of Saragossa; Vincent Pallotti
23 Ildephonsus; John the Almsgiver
24 **Francis of Sales** (*see page 148*)
25 Conversion of **Paul** (*see page 66*); Juventinus and Maximinus
26 Alberic; Eystein; Paula; Timothy and Titus
27 Angela of Brescia
28 Peter Nolasco; **Thomas Aquinas** (*see page 24*)
29 Gildas the Wise; Sulpicius Severus
30 Bathildis; Martina
31 Cyrus and John; **John Bosco** (*see page 152*); Marcella

FEBRUARY

1 **Brigid (Bride)** (*see page 20*)
2 **Blessed Virgin Mary** (Purification) (*see page 12*); Joan of Lestonnac
3 Anskar; **Blaise** (*see page 32*); Ia; Laurence of Canterbury; Werburgh
4 Andrew Corsini; Joan of France; Phileas
5 **Agatha** (*see page 92*)
6 Amand of Maastricht; Dorothy
7 Richard; Theodore the General
8 Cuthman; **Jerome Emiliani** (*see page 26*); John of Matha
9 Apollonia; Nicephorus of Antioch; Teilo
10 Scholastica
11 Benedict of Aniane
12 Julian the Hospitaller; Marina
13 Catherine dei Ricci

14 Cyril and Methodius; Maro; **Valentine** (*see page 44*)
15 Sigfrid
16 Elias and his companions
17 Finan; Fintan of Clonenagh; Seven Servite Founders
18 Colman of Lindisfarne; Flavian of Constantinople
19 Mesrop
20 Shahdost; Ulric of Haselbury
21 Peter Damian
22 Margaret of Cortona
23 Milburga; Polycarp; Willigis
24 Montanus and Lucius
25 Ethelbert of Kent; Walburga
26 Porphyry of Gaza
27 Gabriel Possenti; Leander
28 Oswald of Worcester

MARCH

1 **David** (see page 142)
2 Chad
3 Aelred; Cunegund; **Katharine Drexel** (*see page 85*); Marinus of Caesarea; Winaloe
4 Casimir
5 Kieran of Saighir; Phocas of Antioch; Piran
6 Chrodegang; Colette; Cyneburga
7 Perpetua and Felicity
8 Felix of Dunwich; **John of God** (*see page 119*); Julian of Toledo
9 Catherine of Bologna; **Frances of Rome** (*see page 55*); Gregory of Nyssa
10 John Ogilvie
11 Eulogius of Córdova; Sophronius
12 Maximilian; Simeon the New Theologian
13 Euphrasia; Gerald of Mayo
14 Matilda
15 Clement Hofbauer; **Louise de Marillac** (*see page 150*)
16 Heribert of Cologne; Julian of Antioch; Paul the Simple
17 **Gertrude of Nivelles** (*see page 35*); **Joseph of Arimathea** (*see page 134*); **Patrick** (*see page 33*)
18 Cyril of Jerusalem; Edward the Martyr
19 **Joseph** (as husband of Mary) (*see page 11*)
20 **Cuthbert** (*see page 36*); Herbert of Derwentwater
21 Enda; Nicholas von Flüe
22 Zachary
23 Gwinear; Turibius of Mogrovejo
24 Catherine of Vadstena
25 Alfwold; **Blessed Virgin Mary** (Annunciation) (*see page 12*); Dismas
26 Braulio; Ludger; William of Norwich
27 John the Egyptian; Rupert of Salzburg
28 Alkelda of Middleham
29 Berthold; Jonah and Berikjesu; Mark of Arethusa
30 John Climacus; Osburga

APRIL

1 Hugh of Grenoble
2 Francis of Paola; Mary the Egyptian
3 Pancras of Taormina; Richard of Chichester
4 Benedict the Black; **Isidore of Seville** (*see page 143*)
5 Vincent Ferrer
6 William of Aebelholt
7 **John-Baptist de La Salle** (*see page 151*); Nilus of Sora
8 Perpetuus
9 Waudru
10 Fulbert of Chartres
11 Gemma Galgani; Stanislaus of Cracow
12 Sabas the Goth; Zeno of Verona
13 Carpus and Papylus; Martin I
14 Tiburtius
15 Paternus of Wales
16 Benedict Labre; **Bernadette of Lourdes** (*see page 123*); Magnus of Orkney
17 Donnan; Robert of Chaise-Dieu; Stephen Harding
18 Apollonius; Laserian
19 Elphege; Expeditus; Leo IX
20 Agnes of Montepulciano
21 **Anselm** (*see page 54*); Beuno; Simeon Barsabba'e
22 Conrad of Parzham; Pherbutha; Theodore of Sykeon
23 Adalbert of Prague; **George** (*see page 94*)
24 Euphrasia Pelletier; Ivo; Mellitus
25 **Mark the Evangelist** (*see page 69*); William of Monte Vergine
26 Cletus; Stephen of Perm
27 Maughold; Zita
28 Louis Grignion; Paul of the Cross
29 **Catherine of Siena** (*see page 102*); Hugh of Cluny; Robert of Molesme
30 Joseph Cottonlengo; Marian and James; Pius V

MAY

1 Brieuc; **Joseph ("the Worker")** (*see page 11*)
2 Athanasius
3 Philip and James the Less; Theodosius of the Caves
4 Gothard; Pelagia of Tarsus
5 Hilary of Arles; Jutta
6 **John the Apostle** (West) (*see page 42*)
7 John of Beverley; Lindhard
8 Peter of Tarentaise; Victor
9 Pachomius
10 Antonino; John of Avila
11 Asaph; Comgall; Francis di Girolamo; Mayeul
12 Epiphanius of Salamis; Ignatius of Laconi; Pancras
13 Andrew Fournet; Euthymius the Illuminator
14 Mary Mazzarello; Matthias; Michael Garicoïts
15 Dympna; Hallvard; **Isidore the Farm Laborer** (*see page 145*)
16 **Brendan the Navigator** (*see page 71*); Simon Stock
17 Paschal Baylon
18 Eric; Felix of Cantalice

19 Celestine V; **Dunstan** (*see page 144*); Ives; Joaquina Vedruna de Mas
20 Bernadine of Siena; Ethelbert of East Anglia
21 Godric; **Helen of Constantine** (East) (*see page 45*)
22 **Rita of Cascia** (*see page 118*)
23 Desiderius; Ivo of Chartres; William of Rochester
24 David of Scotland
25 Gregory VII; The Three Marys; **The Venerable Bede** (*see page 52*)
26 Mariana of Quito; Philip Neri
27 **Augustine of Canterbury** (*see page 74*); Julius of Durostorum
28 **Bernard of Aosta** (*see page 99*); Germanus of Paris
29 Bona of Pisa
30 **Ferdinand III of Castile** (*see page 101*); **Joan of Arc** (*see page 104*)
31 Petronella

JUNE

1 Justin; Pamphilus
2 Erasmus (or Elmo); Marcellinus and Peter
3 Clotilda; Kevin
4 Francis Caracciolo; Petroc
5 **Boniface** (*see page 76*)
6 Jarlath of Tuam; **Martha** (East) (*see page 14*); Norbert
7 Meriadoc; Robert of Newminster
8 Melania the Elder; William of York
9 **Columba** (*see page 34*); Pelagia of Antioch
10 Ithamar
11 Barnabas
12 Eskil; John of Sahagun; Leo III
13 **Antony of Padua** (*see page 22*)
14 Methodius of Constantinople
15 **Bernard of Aosta** (*see page 99*); Edburga of Winchester; Germaine of Pibrac; Vitus
16 Cyricus and Julitta; John Regis; Lutgard; Tikhon of Amathus
17 Botolph; Emily de Vialar; Harvey
18 Arnulf of Metz; Elizabeth of Schönau; Mark and Marcellian
19 Gervase and Protase; Juliana Falconieri
20 Adalbert of Magdeburg
21 Aloysius; Méen
22 Alban; John Fisher; **Thomas More** (*see page 56*); Nicetas of Remesiana
23 Etheldreda; Joseph Cafasso
24 **John the Baptist** (Birth) (*see page 108*)
25 Febronia; Prosper of Reggio
26 Anthelm
27 Cyril of Alexandria; Ladislaus
28 Austell; Irenaeus of Lyons
29 **Peter** (*see page 110*) and **Paul** (*see page 66*)
30 Martyrs of Rome; Theobald of Provins

JULY

1 Oliver Plunkett; Aaron and Julius
2 **Blessed Virgin Mary** (Visitation) (*see page 12*); John Francis Regis
3 Leo II; **Thomas the Apostle** (West) (*see page 68*)
4 Andrew of Crete; Ulric of Augsburg
5 Antony of Zaccaria; Athanasius the Athonite; Modwenna
6 Godelive; Maria Goretti; Moninne; Sexburga
7 Ethelburga of Faremoutiers-en-Brie; Hedda; Willibald
8 Elizabeth of Portugal; Procopius
9 Veronica Giuliani
10 Alexander; Amalburga
11 **Benedict** (*see page 50*); Olga
12 John Gualberto; Nabor and Felix; Veronica
13 Eugenius of Carthage; Henry II; Mildred; Silas
14 Camillus; Madelgaire (or Vincent of Soignies)
15 Bonaventure; James of Nisibis; Swithin; **Vladimir of Kiev** (*see page 77*)
16 Helier; Mary-Magdalen Postel; Raineld
17 Alexis; Clement Slovensky; Kenelm; Leo IV
18 Symphorosa and her seven sons
19 Arsenius; Macrina the Younger
20 Margaret of Antioch; Wilgefortis
21 Lawrence of Brindisi; Victor of Marseilles
22 **Mary Magdalene** (*see page 90*)
23 Brigitta of Sweden; John Cassian
24 Boris and Gleb; Christine
25 **Christopher** (see page 70); **James the Greater** (*see page 64*)
26 Joachim and **Anne** (*see page 10*)
27 Aurelius and Natalia; Celestine I
28 Nazarius and Celsus; Samson
29 Lupus of Troyes; **Martha** (West) (*see page 14*); Olaf
30 Justin de Jacobis; Peter Chrysologus
31 Germanus of Auxerre; **Ignatius Loyola** (*see page 58*)

AUGUST

1 Alphonsus Liguori; Ethelwold
2 Basil the Blessed; Eusebius of Vercelli
3 Peter Julian Eymard
4 John-Baptist Vianney
5 Afra; Cassyon
6 Donatus; Justus and Paster
7 Cajetan; Sixtus II and his companions; Victricius
8 Cyriacus; **Dominic** (*see page 80*); Hormisdas
9 Oswald of Northumbria
10 Lawrence
11 Attractra; Blaan; **Clare of Assisi** (*see page 23*); Susanna; Tiburtius
12 Jambert, Murtagh
13 Cassian of Imola; Radegund
14 **Maximilian Kolbe**(*see page 124*)

15 **Blessed Virgin Mary** (Assumption) (*see page 12*); Tarsicius
16 Roch; Stephen of Hungary
17 Hyacinth of Cracow; Clare of Montefalco
18 Florus and Laurus; **Helen of Constantine** (West) (*see page 45*)
19 John Eudes
20 Armadour; **Bernard of Clairvaux** (*see page 78*); Oswain; Philibert
21 Abraham of Smolensk; **Pius X** (*see page 105*); Sidonius Apollinaris
22 Symphorian
23 Philip Benizi; Rose of Lima
24 Bartholomew; Jane Antide Thouret; Ouen
25 Genesius of Arles; Gregory of Utrecht; Louis IX
26 Elizabeth Bichier des Âges
27 Caesarius of Arles; **Monica** (*see page 15*)
28 **Augustine** (*see page 140*); Hermes
29 **John the Baptist** (Death) (*see page 108*); Sebbi
30 Felix and Adauctus; Pammachius
31 Aidan of Lindisfarne; Raymund Nonnatus

SEPTEMBER

1 **Giles** (*see page 37*); **Simeon the Stylite** (East) (*see page 49*)
2 Brocard
3 Cuthburga; **Gregory the Great** (*see page 72*)
4 Marinus of San Marino; Ultan
5 Bertin; Lawrence Guistiniani
6 Cagnoald
7 Cloud; Evurtius
8 **Blessed Virgin Mary** (Nativity) (*see page 12*); Adrian
9 Isaac the Great; Peter Claver
10 Finian of Moville; Nicholas of Tolentino
11 Deiniol; Protus and Hyacinthus
12 Ailbe; Guy of Anderlecht
13 **John Chrysostom** (West) (*see page 48*)
14 The Holy Cross
15 Catherine of Genoa
16 Cornelius and Cyprian; Edith of Wilton; Ninian
17 Hildegard; Robert Bellarmino
18 **Joseph of Cupertino** (*see page 84*)
19 **Januarius** (*see page 93*); Theodore of Canterbury
20 Eustace; Korean Martyrs
21 **Matthew** (*see page 128*)
22 Thomas of Villanova
23 Adamnan; **Padre Pio** (*see page 125*); Thecla
24 Gerard
25 Cadoc; Finbar; Florence
26 Cosmas and Damian; **John the Apostle** (East) (*see page 42*); Nilus
27 **Vincent de Paul** (*see page 61*)
28 Lioba; Wenceslas
29 **Michael the Archangel** (*see page 88*); Gabriel; Raphael and all angels
30 Honorius; **Jerome** (*see page 138*)

OCTOBER

1 Bavo; **Teresa of Lisieux** (*see page 154*)
2 Guardian Angels; Leger
3 Ewalds
4 **Francis of Assisi** (*see page 38*)
5 Mauras and Placid
6 Bruno; Faith; **Thomas the Apostle** (East) (*see page 68*)
7 Justina; Osyth
8 Demetrius; Pelagia
9 Denis; John Leonardi; Louis Bertrand
10 Francis Borgia; Paulinus of York
11 Alexander Sauli; Canice
12 Edwin; Wilfred
13 **Edward the Confessor** (*see page 98*); Gerald of Aurillac
14 Callistus; Justus of Lyons
15 Albert; **Teresa of Avila** (*see page 120*)
16 Gall; **Gerard Majella** (*see page 27*); Margaret Mary Alacoque
17 **Ignatius of Antioch** (*see page 113*)
18 Justus of Beauvias; **Luke** (*see page 132*)
19 Jean de Brébeuf and Isaac Joques; Frideswide
20 Andrew of Crete; Maria Boscardin
21 Hilarion; Ursula
22 Donatus; Philip of Heraclea
23 Ignatius of Constantinople; John of Capestrano
24 Antony Claret; Felix of Thibiuca
25 Crispin and Crispinian; **Edmund Campion** (*see page 81*)
26 Bean; Cedd; Eata
27 Frumentius; Odran
28 **Jude** (*see page 112*) and Simon
29 Colman of Kilmacduagh
30 Alphonsus Rogriquez; Marcellus the Centurion
31 Foillian; Wolfgang

NOVEMBER

1 All Saints; Benignus
2 All Souls; Justus of Trieste
3 Hubert; **Malachy of Armagh** (*see page 100*); **Martin de Porres** (*see page 60*)
4 Charles Borromeo; Emeric
5 Zachary and Elizabeth
6 Illtyd; Leonard; Winnoc
7 Congar; Willibrord
8 Cuby; Willehad
9 Theodore
10 Andrew Avellino; **Leo the Great** (*see page 96*)
11 **Martin of Tours** (*see page 137*); Theodore the Studite
12 Josephat; Lebuin
13 Frances Cabrini; **John Chrysostom** (East) (*see page 48*); Stanislaus Kostka
14 Gregory Palamas; Laurence O'Toole
15 **Albert the Great** (see page 146); Fintan of Rheinau; Leopold of Austria
16 Edmund of Abingdon; Gertrude; Margaret of Scotland
17 **Elizabeth of Hungary** (*see page 21*); Hilda; Hugh of Lincoln
18 Mawes; Odo of Cluny

19 Barlaam of Antioch; Ermenburga
20 Bernward; Edmund
21 Gelasius I; Condedus
22 **Cecilia** (*see page 136*); Philemon and Apphia
23 Clement; **Columban** (*see page 75*)
24 Chrysogonus; Colman of Cloyne
25 **Catherine of Alexandria** (formerly) (*see page 115*)
26 John Berchmans; Leonard of Port Maurice
27 Fergus; Virgil of Salzburg
28 Catherine Labouré; James of the March
29 Brendan of Birr
30 **Andrew** (*see page 130*)

DECEMBER

1 Eligius; Natalia
2 Viviana
3 **Francis Xavier** (*see page 82*)
4 Barbara; John of Damascus
5 Crispina
6 **Nicholas of Myra** (*see page 16*)
7 **Ambrose** (*see page 18*)
8 Budoc
9 Leocadia; Peter Fourier
10 Eulalia; Miltiades
11 Damasus I; Daniel the Stylite
12 Finnian of Clonard; Jeanne Chantal
13 Judoc; Lucy
14 Fingar; **John of the Cross** (*see page 122*)
15 Mary di Rosa; Offa of Essex
16 Adelaide; Bean
17 Begga; Lazarus; Olympias
18 Flannan; Winnibald
19 Urban V
20 Dominic of Silos
21 Peter Canisius
22 Chaeremon and Ischyrion
23 Frithbert; John of Kanti Thorlac
24 Charbel Makhlouf
25 Anastasia; Eugenia
26 **Stephen** (*see page 109*)
27 Fabiola; **John the Apostle** (West) (*see page 42*)
28 Holy Innocents
29 **Thomas à Becket** (*see page 116*)
30 Egwin
31 Sylvester

Name Index

Subject Index

BIBLIOGRAPHY

Athanasius, St., *The Life of Antony* (trans. Mayer, R., Ancient Christian Writers), 1950

Attwater, D., *The Penguin Dictionary of Saints*, 1965

Augustine of Hippo, St., *Confessions* (trans.), 1923

Baynes, N., *Byzantium*, 1948

Bettenson, H. (ed.), *The Early Christian Fathers*, 1956

Bettenson, H. (ed.), *The Later Christian Fathers*, 1970

Chadwick, O., *The Reformation* (The Penguin History of the Church, vol. 3), 1964

Coulton, G., *A Medieval Garner*, 1928

Farmer, D., *The Oxford Dictionary of Saints*, 1978

Gascoigne, B., *The Christians*, 1977

Hamon, A., *The Life of St. Francis de Sales* (2 vols, 1925–29)

Ignatius Loyola, St., *Autobiography* (trans. O'Callaghan, J.,) 1974

Knowles, D., *Thomas Becket*, 1970

McManners, J. (ed.), *The Oxford Illustrated History of Christianity*, 1990

Neill, S., *A History of Christian Missions* (The Penguin History of the Church, vol. 6), 1964

Pastor, L. (Baron) von, *History of the Popes from the Close of the Middle Ages*, 1933

Reed, O., *An Illustrated History of Saints and Symbols*

Southern, R., *Western Society and the Church in the Middle Ages* (The Penguin History of the Church, vol. 2), 1970

Stevenson, J. (ed.), *A New Eusebius*, 1957

Stevenson, J. (ed.), *Creeds, Councils, and Controversies*, 1966

Teresa of Lisieux, St., *The Story of A Soul*, 1898

Walsh, M. (ed.), *Butler's Lives of the Saints*, 1985

CREDITS